EVERNOTE

From Note Taking to Life Mastery

100 Eye-Opening Techniques and Sneaky Uses of Evernote that Experts Don't Want You to Know

By John Scott

First Printing, 2017 - Printed in the United States of America

Every day we are bombarded with more things to remember and more activities and tasks to complete. More, more, more. It can often reach a point where there is so much information coming at you that you have no clue where to start or what actually needs doing. It's simply overwhelming. There is hope.

TABLE OF CONTENTS

INTRODUCTION

No matter what you're currently doing with your life – whether you're starting your own business, you're a student or you're a working mum – **it can be _really_ challenging to keep track of everything**. We're all just so…busy! With a **constant and ever-growing to-do list**, it's no wonder things are getting forgotten, misplaced, or even just a bit overwhelming.

Well, now there is a **solution to all of your problems**!

Now, you're probably thinking _'I've heard all of that before. Every supposed 'solution' to my problems just ends up causing me more work!'_ Well, that's where Evernote is different. **Evernote** is a simple to use system, which cleverly converts everything you are already doing into a way that **assists you in taking control of your life**.

Evernote is the revolutionary application which allows you to store all of your documentation in one place. This can then all be accessed from absolutely anywhere, using your PC (_Mac_ or _Windows_), laptop, tablet or even your mobile phone (_Android_ or _iOs_). This cross-platform app **_serves many purposes from simple note-taking to coordinating an entire work project_** involving many different people. This means that if you'll let it, it can help run your entire life – **it can become your new PA**!

The many features of Evernote are **designed** with one simple goal in mind – **to make your life easier**. Not only does it assist you in managing your time, it keeps everything together in one place. This means that you can use it for absolutely everything, dividing it all up into manageable sections so nothing gets confused –*business; research, writing, school, finances* and even *personal use at home*. In fact, there isn't a single person who won't benefit from using it – especially as it fits in around you and your lifestyle with ease. Not only will Evernote help save you time, it'll free up all of your space by allowing you to store everything electronically, which you can then access wherever you are.

This guide will **help you learn** the ins and outs, tips and tricks, secrets and backdoor hacks that you will find nowhere else on the internet. It no longer has to be difficult to take down your thoughts, make to-do lists, and so much more.

Whether you personally decide to use the *free, premium* or the *business version* of Evernote depends on what you require it for. The free version has a very lot of useful features, including monthly uploads of 60MB and the ability to share your notes, but if you are going to use it comprehensively for your business, it might be worth looking into the premium or business options. These offer more monthly uploads, offline notebooks, pin lock and the ability for others to edit any notes that you share. As Evernote is likely to become a staple app that you use very regularly, on a daily basis, these extra features may prove extremely useful to you.

It may not surprise you to learn that today there are over 200 million (and growing) Evernote users worldwide, but you may be shocked to learn that **over 1.4 million** of these **choose the premium services (as of 2012)** – this number alone shows how much people value the extra features offered.

There are many *reasons that people choose to use Evernote* to help them with the day-to-day running of their lives, and the Top reasons include:

- **Travel** – Evernote makes it very easy to continue to run your business whilst you are on the move. Not only will you have all of your work documents stored in one place which you can access wherever you are, but you can also keep your travel information safe, keep track of any expenses you have incurred, and keep in touch with everyone back I the office about a project you're involved with.

- **Multi-purpose Notes** – The 'Notes' that you will go on to create don't just have to include text. Pictures, video and audio are just a few of the useful features that will make your life easier.

- **Tailored Use** – Everyone uses Evernote differently and for varying reasons. The *way* you use the app, and the add-on features that you select to work alongside it, will make it work exactly as *you* want it to.

- **Go Paperless** – It's a great way to 'go paperless'. We all want to stop wasting the Earth's resources and reduce our carbon footprint – and using Evernote instead of a notepad is a great way to start.

- **Ease of Use** – Finally, Evernote is extremely simple to use, but can do some *really* complex things that will make your life *so* much easier. You will learn about these tricks throughout this book.

Of course, this is just a few of the many, *many* reasons; there are so many advantages to using Evernote, which will be examined in much more detail throughout this guide, but one thing is for sure...downloading **Evernote will revolutionize the way you run your day-to-day life**, making you wonder what you ever did without it! The number of users increases on a daily basis as more and more people realize how useful Evernote is. This popularity shows that Evernote is far more than just a phase – it's a revolution, and one that you don't want to miss out on!

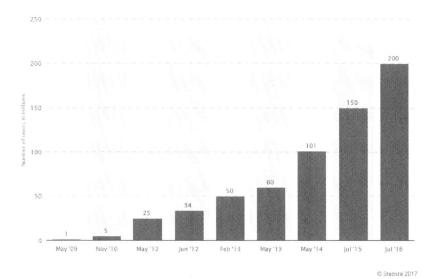

Evernote user growth as of 2017

Region	Users (Millions)
Asia Pacific	35
Europe, Middle East, Africa	31
US and Canada	27
Latin America	8
Total users	101

Evernote users as of 2014

SIMPLE STEPS FOR GETTING STARTED

So now that you have decided to use Evernote, **how do you go about getting started?** This chapter will give you all the basics; setting up an account, notes, note types and notebooks. Once you have worked through all of this, working your way around Evernote will be simple – then we will get to the more interesting ways Evernote can help you!

SETTING UP AN ACCOUNT

Setting up an account with Evernote is so simple and only takes a few seconds – so there is certainly no reason not to at least give it a try! First you need to log on to *Evernote* at www.evernote.com/Registration.action and create new account by filling up this form:

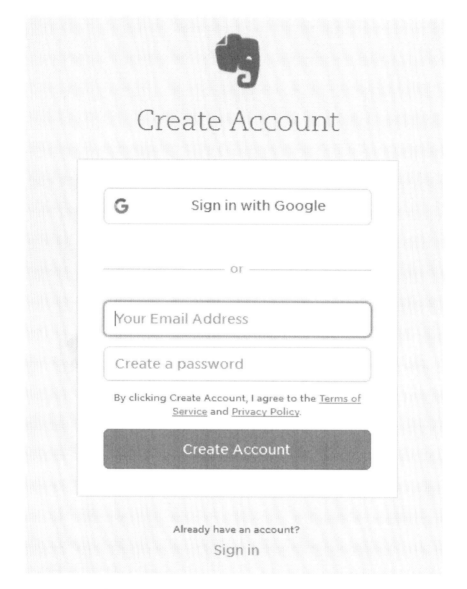

Here you need to enter your email address and the password you wish to use for your account (be sure to use a secure password as Evernote will eventually hold *all* of your important – and possible sensitive – documents). After you have entered this information to the relevant boxes, click 'Create Account'...

...and that's it!

It couldn't be simpler, and as Evernote is actually available in a wide range of languages, including *English, Spanish, French, German, Dutch, Portuguese, Chinese, Russian, Japanese* and *Italian* to name just a few, there is really nothing stopping you!

The next screen that you will come across will be the ***Evernote home screen*** – this will become **very** familiar to you the more you use the application as it is where you will always end up first.

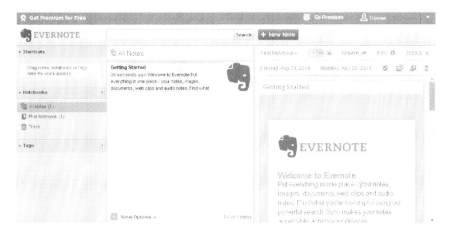

A Quick Dashboard Tour for Evernote Web interface

- In the top menu bar you have a menu with your account information on the right-hand side.

- In about the center of the top menu we have the New Note selection with the plus sign for adding new notes, then finally, the ever powerful search bar.

- On the left panel, you can find Shortcuts, the Notebooks view option and the Tags view option. Shortcuts let you store shortcuts to the notes you access on a regular basis. Notebooks area lists your Notebooks and Notebook stacks. You can also hide all unused Tags from the Tags area by right clicking on Tags and selecting *Hide Unassigned Tags.*

You can then start to experiment with all the features that Evernote has to offer you. Be sure to play around with your mobile device to learn your way around version of Evernote, too!

It is advisable to also download the Evernote App onto your mobile phone, tablet and even onto your desktop to make using Evernote easier, more efficient and more accessible wherever you are by using the same log in details. This can be found in the *Android* or *iOs* store.

On your mobile devices, the free Evernote app will be available in your App store and you just download it in the same way you would any other application. It will be easily recognizable by the **elephant logo** (because of course, an *elephant never forgets!*)

To download it onto Windows, you click on the '*Download*' button on the home screen.

And then follow the instructions...

(The Mac set-up is very similar)

Downloading Evernote
for Windows

If your download didn't start, click here.

1. Download and Install

Click the Evernote file in the lower left corner of your browser window.

2. Run the installer

Follow the steps in the installer. It only takes a minute.

3. Get Started

Launch Evernote and create your first note!

Having Evernote available on all of your devices means that you will use it more, and as you will learn through the rest of this book the more you use it, the more useful it will become.

4 WAYS YOU CAN USE NOTES

Notes are the staple feature of Evernote. They are there for you to create documents, to-do lists, save ideas...anything you need them for! This is likely to become your **most used Evernote feature**, so it's a good idea to familiarize yourself with how to use them effectively!

To create a note, you first need to click on the 'New Note' button which can be found on your home screen.

This will then open a new 'Note' screen where you can start typing.

The list of your notes will be on the left-hand side of the screen. Your new note will automatically be called '*Untitled*' until you fill in the title box on the right-hand side of the screen. Be sure to **give the note a name which will allow you to refer to it** and access it easily. '*Note#1*' will not be useful at a later date when you're trying to find what you had written down!

Once you start typing in the **Note box**, all the text features will pop up, allowing you to edit your writing to suit your personal needs.

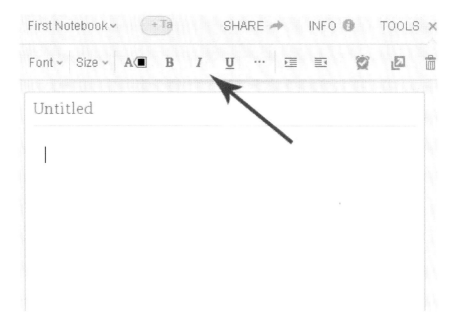

It is very likely that you are used to using this style of editing from Word programmes, but if not, here is a little guideline for you of each item:

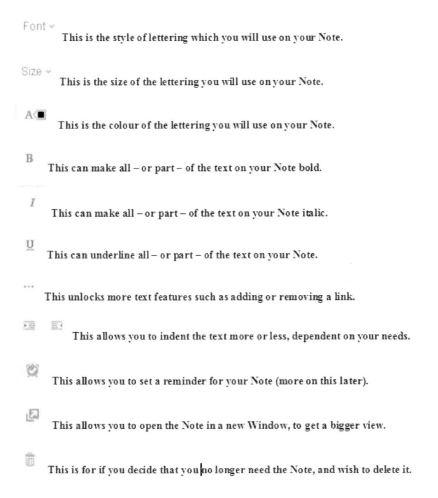

This is the style of lettering which you will use on your Note.

This is the size of the lettering you will use on your Note.

This is the colour of the lettering you will use on your Note.

This can make all – or part – of the text on your Note bold.

This can make all – or part – of the text on your Note italic.

This can underline all – or part – of the text on your Note.

This unlocks more text features such as adding or removing a link.

This allows you to indent the text more or less, dependent on your needs.

This allows you to set a reminder for your Note (more on this later).

This allows you to open the Note in a new Window, to get a bigger view.

This is for if you decide that you no longer need the Note, and wish to delete it.

Once you have written your **Note**, you may wish to **SHARE** it. This could be with work colleagues or friends and family.

To do this, simply click on the '*Share*' button at the top of the Note on the right hand side of the screen, and a dropdown menu of share options will appear.

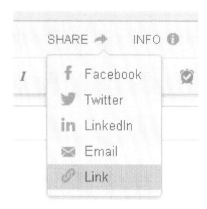

If you select one of the social media options for sharing, this warning message will appear to let you know that the Note will become public and can be viewed by anyone, not just Evernote users. If you are happy with this, simply click 'OK'...it couldn't be any easier!

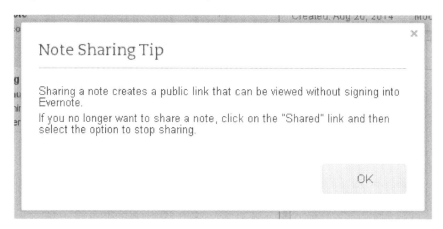

If you decide to send the Note via email, to specific people, then it will become public to them (and the people they decide to share it with). This box will appear after you click on the *'Email'* selection, allowing you to fill in the required details.

As you can see, if you have a Gmail account, you can *import all of your email contacts* saving you having to type them in every single time, to make the process much easier and quicker for you, particularly if you are using Evernote for all of your business needs.

You also have the option of *getting the link for your Note*, if you would like to share it that way.

Another wonderful thing about Evernote is that it allows you to **MERGE multiple documents** into one, making it more proficient. This means you can combine your images into your word documents, or merge the work of two or more people to complete a project.

You can merge your notes by selecting the notes that you wish to combine on the list on the left-hand side of the screen. You can do this by holding down *Command* and *left-clicking* on Mac and *Ctrl* and *left-clicking* on PC. Thumbnails of the documents with options on the right hand side of the screen.

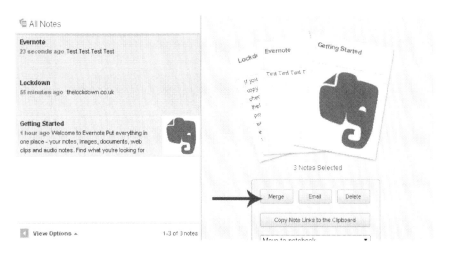

Click on the '*Merge*' buttons, which will come up with a warning message, if this is all acceptable, click 'Merge'.

Merging these notes will make them unavailable to specialized Evernote applications.

Cancel   Merge

These documents will then become one. If you are a Mac user, the new document will take the name of the most recently modified Note. If you are a PC user, it will use the name of the earliest Note – you can change the name in the title bar if necessary.

For one reason or another, you may wish to **DELETE a Note** – once it has served its purpose, there is no point in it clogging up your home page! So just as you'd cross an item off a to-do list, you can dispose of a Note.

To do this, you can either use the icon above the Note on the right-hand side of the screen that has been previously discussed in this chapter...

...or right click on the Note you wish to get rid of on the list which is found on the left-hand side of the screen.

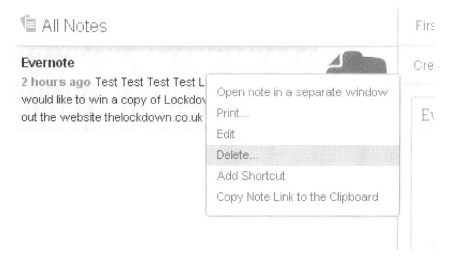

Choose '*Delete*' from the drop down menu. You will then be given a warning message, just to confirm that you aren't deleting anything by mistake!

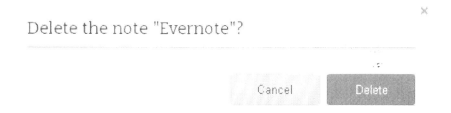

If you want to recover a deleted note, simply go to Trash, select the Note and click "Restore Note".

It really is as easy as that! This is so much simpler and less time consuming as writing down notes in a notepad, and it saves you having to carry one around with you as well! It is very likely that you will always have your mobile phone with you anyway, so wouldn't it be much more convenient if all your notes were on there too?

So now that you have seen the basic things that you can do with your notes, it's time to look at the different types of notes you can create – and this is where it gets more exciting!

NOTE TYPES – HOW TO
MAKE THE MOST OF EACH

One of the ways Evernote stands out as such a useful, life enhancing app is the fact that it doesn't just take written notes. There are many different ways you can save the information you need, and here is how to do so.

Audio

There are many different reasons that you may wish to record an audio note – the minutes of a meeting, a class lecture, a speech that you need to remember, or even something musical. Whatever the reason, it's a simple and easy process which may just save you a lot of time.

Using the desktop Evernote app, you start by clicking on the dropdown menu next to the '*New Note*' option, and then you choose '*New Audio Note*' from the list.

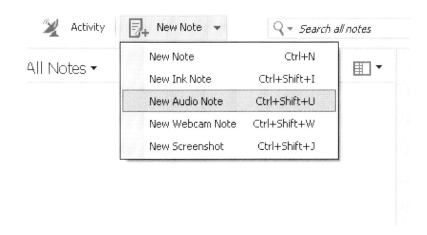

This will bring up the *Audio Note screen*. As you can see from the image below, notes containing audio can also contain text with all the formatting of a regular Note. You can also have multiple audio tracks within a Note, saving you time and space. You can be much more organized with all the relevant audio kept within one place.

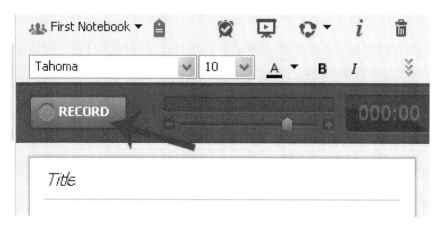

Once you are ready, hit the '*Record*' button and Evernote will begin copying all the audio that you require. The blue 'sound' line will flicker so you know that Evernote is picking everything up alright.

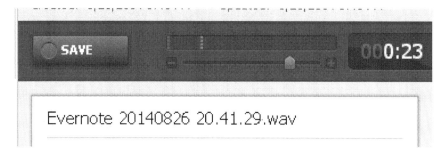

Once you have got all of the audio you need, simply hit the '*Save*' button and that will finish the Note. Just remember that you *can* type while the audio is recording, but if you click off the Note, it will stop recording.

This is slightly different on other formats of the app, but the principle is the same:

- *For iOs devices*, you tap the paperclip icon – which is located on the bottom bar – and then 'Audio' to start recording the note, and 'Done' when you're finished.

- *For Android devices*, you tap the '+' icon on the top bar, fol-lowed by 'Record Audio'. When you're done, click the checkmark icon on the top left. This will stop recording and save the note.

- *Windows Phones* have a microphone symbol on the Evernote home screen, which you tap to start recording in a quick note. If you want to record in a Note you have already started, click the same symbol on the bottom bar. Click the checkmark to end re-cording and save the Note.

Webcam

Including webcam in your notes is a fantastic feature which allows you to include snapshots. This can assist you in many ways; a picture of a business card, the label of a wine bottle you particularly enjoyed, a photo of a family moment you'd like to capture...the possibilities are endless.

To include a webcam image within your Note, start by selecting a 'New Webcam Note' from the 'New Note' dropdown menu.

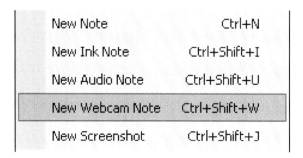

This will produce a webcam box above your Note.

The image from your webcam will appear inside this box (the Evernote logo has only been used as an example). You then click on the 'Take Snapshot' button to capture the relevant image.

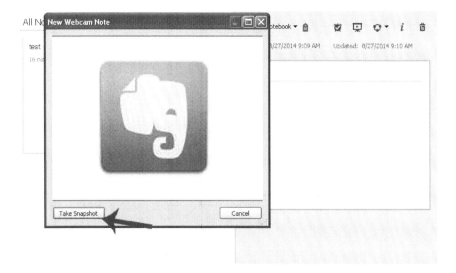

This will then give you the option to 'Cancel', 'Retake Snapshot' or 'Save to

Evernote'. Once you are happy with the image you have captured, and saved it, you will return to the Note screen.

If you want to add any text to your webcam note, simply click on the '*Annotate*' button, which appears when you hover the mouse over the large Note image on the right-hand side of the screen.

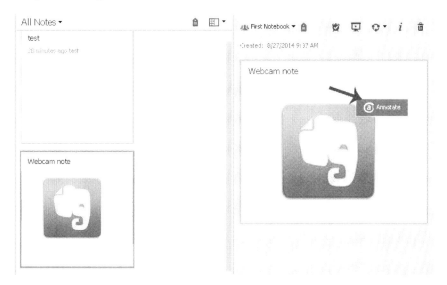

This will bring up another box, which not only allows you to add text, but gives you a whole range of options to annotate your image – all of which are noted on the image below. As you can see, you can edit your webcam note to suit your individual needs.

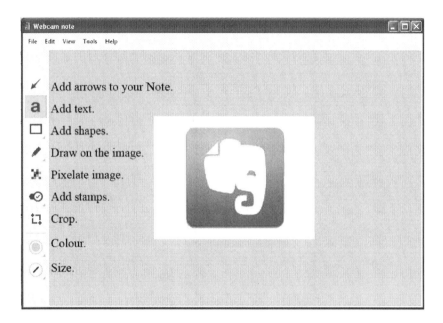

Then you simply click '*File*' at the top left-hand side of the box, and '*Save and Exit*'.

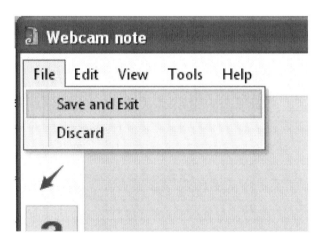

On other formats, this is very similar to the Audio Note section. The webcam symbol is labeled clearly.

Ink

Ink Notes have been designed so you can hand write or draw your notes, in the same way you might do in a paper notepad. These start in the same way as audio and webcam notes, by selecting the '*New Note*' and choosing '*New Ink Note*' from the dropdown menu.

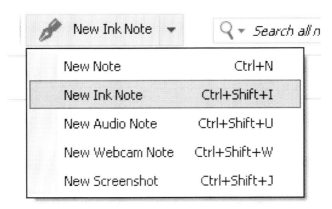

This will then bring you to a screen with lined paper with which you can use the mouse (or your finger if you're using a touch screen device) to write your message or draw your note – which is extremely useful to those in the graphics industry.

There are tools on the Ink Note which allow you to add some variety to your written or drawn piece.

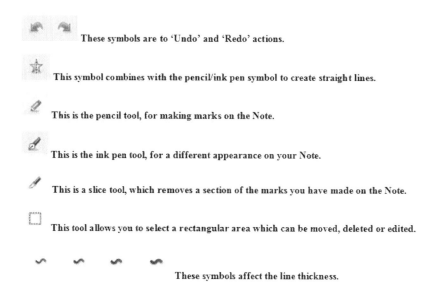

These symbols are to 'Undo' and 'Redo' actions.

This symbol combines with the pencil/ink pen symbol to create straight lines.

This is the pencil tool, for making marks on the Note.

This is the ink pen tool, for a different appearance on your Note.

This is a slice tool, which removes a section of the marks you have made on the Note.

This tool allows you to select a rectangular area which can be moved, deleted or edited.

These symbols affect the line thickness.

The color wheel symbol is to change the color of your work.

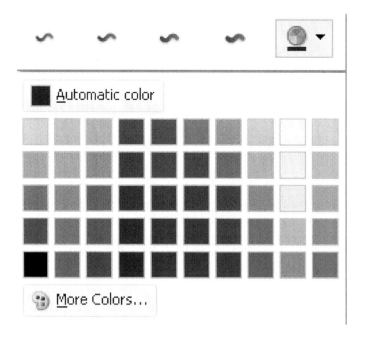

Once you have created your Ink Note, it will save automatically, just as any other Note and can be accessed from any of your devices.

Screenshot

A Screenshot Note is different to a Webcam Note because it is adding images from the computer screen, rather than a photograph. To do this, you first need to select '*New Screenshot*' from the '*New Note*' dropdown menu.

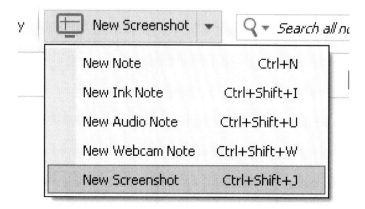

This will bring up a horizontal and vertical line crossing the screen, with the message shown below, which effectively informs you to click where you'd like the screenshot to be created (just be sure to have the screen that you wish to Screenshot open).

A box will appear with your screenshot, giving you the same options as the webcam note did (i.e. text, shapes, pixilation, etc). Once you have finished any edits, click '*File*' in the top left-hand corner and '*Save and Exit*' which will bring you back to the normal Evernote home screen.

Reading all of this information about notes might make you start to wonder about your data. After all, if you're intending to use this application for not only your personal information, but all of your business documents too, how do you know **how safe it is?**

Evernote has this covered. They have, what they refer to as, the '*3 Laws of Data Protection*'.

- **Your data is yours** – Evernote stake **no** claim whatsoever on the information that you enter into it's system. It all belongs to you.

- **Your data is protected** – Everything is private by default. Evernote is not interested in making money from your data. You can *choose* to allow others to see what you have saved, but this will not be done without your consent. Your data is also protected from accidental loss and theft. Evernote holds many redundant central servers to keep a copy of your information, *just in case this happens.*

- **Your data is portable** – Not only is it easy to sign up with Evernote and store all of your data, it is also just as easy to remove everything and close down your account. There is no legal data lock-in, Evernote wants you to stay because you *want* to, not because you have to.

5 WAYS NOTEBOOKS CAN ORGANIZE YOUR LIFE

Notebooks are a fantastic way to **organize all of your notes**. Whether you are using Evernote for business or pleasure, notebooks will become a way for you to keep track of everything. They are easy to use, simple to organize and will make your life so much less stressful. For example, you may have *'Work Notes'* and *'Personal Notes'* or *'Project 1'* etc.

Evernote will automatically create you a Notebook when you open your account. This will be called *'First Notebook'* and will contain *all* your notes. For this reason, many people rename it to *"Inbox"* (with the quote symbols included) so that it always stays at the top of the list of your Notebooks, and because everything ends up in there so it is effectively a little like an inbox – of course, this isn't something you have to do, you can name and use your default Notebook in any way you chose. Part of the beauty of Evernote is that you can use it in the way which benefits you best.

To create a new Notebook, either right-click (PC) or control-click (MAC) in the sidebar, which will give you the option to *'Create Notebook'*.

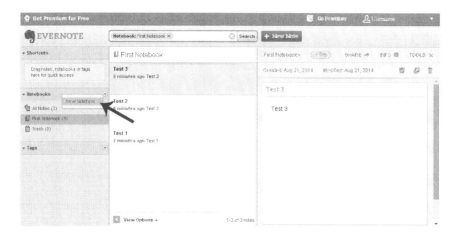

This will immediately give you the chance to name your Notebook. Don't forget to **give it a name which clearly states what Notes are kept in it** – to save confusion at a later date.

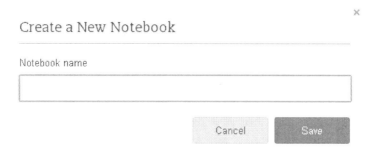

Now that your Notebook has been created, you can start **adding Notes** immediately. You can either left-click on the Note and drag it to the sidebar to drop it into the relevant Notebook. Or, if you'd prefer to do a few at a time, select the notes that you wish to add to the Notebook on the list on the left-hand side of the screen. You can do this by holding down *Command* and left-clicking on Mac and *Ctrl* and left-clicking on PC. Thumbnails of the documents with options on the right hand side of the screen.

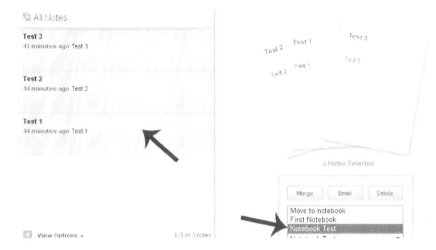

Then you'll want to click on the '*Move to Notebook*' dropdown menu, and select the Notebook you wish your Notes to be saved in. The Notes will be moved for you, and they'll stay there until you move or delete them.

If you decide to **delete a Notebook**, all the Notes within it will be moved to the Trash folder. To perform a deletion, you need to use the sidebar and either right-click (PC) or control-click (MAC) on the Notebook you wish to delete to bring up a drop down menu.

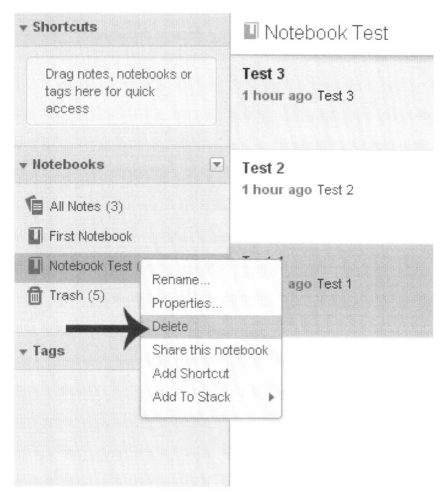

Clicking '*Delete*' will cause the following warning message to appear...just to confirm that you aren't deleting something by mistake!

×

Delete notebook?

Permanently deleting "Notebook Test". 3 active notes will be moved to the trash. This operation cannot be undone.

Cancel   Delete

You may also wish to **share your Notebook**, with colleagues or friends and family.

To do this, simply right-click (PC) or control-click (MAC) on your chosen Notebook on the sidebar, which will bring up a dropdown menu.

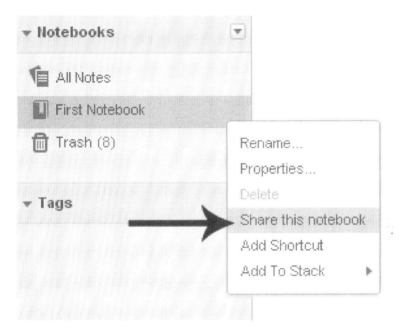

Select '*Share this Notebook*' which will bring up the following selection box.

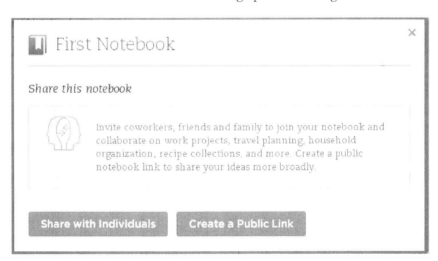

Then depending on what you wish to do, you can select '*Share with Individuals*' which will provide you with the following option, so you can email the correct people – again having a Gmail account provides you with a time saving advantage here as your contacts can be quickly imported, saving you having to type in all the relevant email addresses.

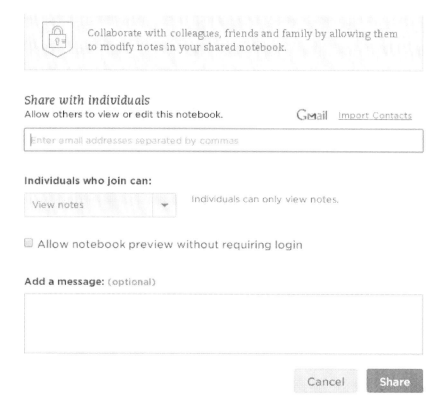

If the information is something that you'd like to be made available to everyone, then you'll want to choose '*Create a Public Link*'. This will cause a pop up box with a link for you to copy and paste on your website, social media...wherever you'd like it to be displayed.

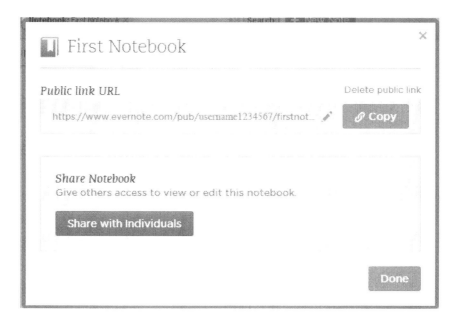

There are many ways to organize your Notebooks to make them much easier to use and locate at a later date. You may wish to **group a certain set of Notebooks** together, for instance you may want to have a collection for 'Work', which a separate notebook for each client or project. This is called a **'Stack'**.

To create a Stack, you can either click on a Notebook and drag it on top of another, or you can right-click on the Notebook and select '*Add to Stack*' from the dropdown menu, which will produce a list of Stacks so you can chose the right one.

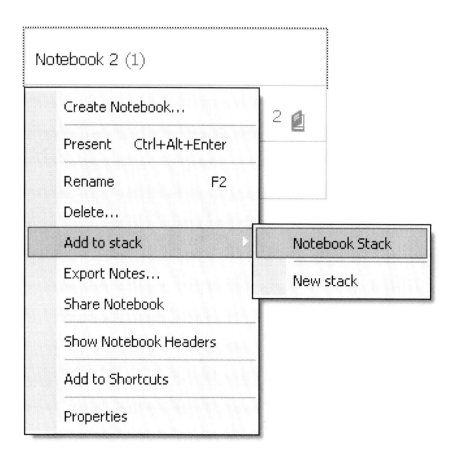

Whichever option you choose, the Stacks will contain a list of Notebooks that sit within them.

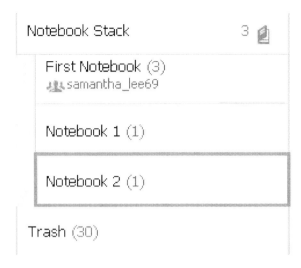

You can rename (or even delete) your Stack by right-clicking on it and selecting the appropriate option.

Just remember that **Stacks cannot be shared**, but the individual Notebooks within them can. Although Stacks can only be created in the desktop version of Evernote, they can be accessed through any device.

There is also an additional way to organize your Notebooks, which is referred to in Evernote as '**Tags**'. These are **keywords that are associated with the Note** to allow you to find the necessary information from a quick search – saving you the time and effort of hunting through all of your notes and notebooks manually.

To add a Tag to a Note, use the toolbar at the top of the note editor section, on the right-hand side of the screen. There is a '+ Tag' box, which you need to left-click in and start typing.

This is the desktop version of Evernote. On other formats, you may need to select 'More' or '...' to find the '*Add Tag*' button. Tags suggested from previous keywords you have used will appear, so if you are trying to group some things, you will only need to spend the time typing the word out once.

When searching through your Tags, Evernote will look through all of your

Notebooks and Stacks, saving you lots of time and energy. It does the hard work for you.

THE EVERNOTE PACKAGES

EVERNOTE
Free

EVERNOTE
Premium

EVERNOTE
Business

All the basic features discussed, are available on the **free Evernote package**, but does that make it the right one for you to choose? There are many things you need to consider when deciding this. Although the basic Evernote can work around you, **your personal needs may actually require the premium or business version** of the application.

As you can see from the chart below, the package that you choose can give you exactly what you need. It may be worth spending the money if some of the extra features are important to you. For example, if you need to create a huge amount of notes to organize your life, *the business option* which gives you up to 500,000 notes with up to 100MB note size, and up to 250 notebooks and stacks, is going to be more beneficial. *The premium features* also give you more security so you will need to consider exactly how sensitive your data is.

If your Evernote account and usage is purely for you then *the free version* of it will suffice, but if you are going to want to collaborate with other employees, then premium and business offer you the chance to not only share notes, but edit them as well. The more you spend on your account, the quicker you will get assistance from the Evernote help team. This may or may not be of importance to you – as with all the Evernote features, it is something specifically personalized to you.

	Free	Premium	Business
Access to all versions of Evernote	Yes	Yes	Yes
Synchronization across platforms	Yes	Yes	Yes
Text Recognition inside images	Yes	Yes	Yes
Note allowance	Unlimited storage, Upload 40MB p/m.	Unlimited storage, Upload 1GB p/m	Unlimited storage, Upload 2GB p/m
File synchronization	Limited: images, audio, ink, PDF.	Any file type.	Any file type.
Search within PDF's	No	Yes	Yes
Access to Note history	No	Yes	Yes
Offline Notebooks	No	Yes	Yes
Notebook sharing	Read Only	Read and Edit	Read and Edit
Joined Notebooks	100	100	250
Notebooks and Stacks	1 – 250	1 – 250	1 – 5,000
Maximum number of Notes	100,000	100,000	500,000
Max single Note size	25MB	50MB	100MB
Support	Standard	Premium	Highest level
Security Features	Standard	SSL Encryption	SSL Encryption
Priority Image Recognition	No	Yes	Yes
Hide promotions	No	Yes	Yes
Cost	Free	£4 per month	£8 per month

So as you can see, the higher the package you chose, the more useful Evernote will become.

Note that you can have up to 100,000 Tags per any Evernote account, so make sure to make the most of them.

TIP: Having an access to Note history (only available for Premium and Business) might be vitally important especially if you delete or modify the note accidentally.

You might start off thinking that the free version of Evernote is all you will ever need – most people do – but 22% of people *do* end up upgrading so it is best for you to be aware of all the premium services offer in case you do decide to make the jump for yourself!

50 PROVEN TIPS
FOR BEGINNERS

Here is an overview of all the **Evernote advices for beginners**. These will assist you on getting started with Evernote.

1. If you download the Evernote app to *all* of your devices, you never need to be without it. You can always access and save stuff to it. Evernote can become your '*External Brain*' – remembering and organizing everything for you, so you don't have to. You won't have to ask "Where did I put that?" again. If the unthinkable should happen and you find yourself without *any* of your electronic devices, don't forget that you can access your information from any computer – just be careful to log out after you have finished.

2. If you keep your '*To Do*' list as one of your Evernote Notes, you can access it all the time, meaning you will never forget anything, or miss an important deadline, ever again.

3. Working with others on a school or work project, won't ever have to be an issue again! Just create your own Notes separately and *Merge* them once you are finished – allowing Evernote to save you time and effort. Don't forget to highlight the most important information in your Notes. Teachers often use **Shared Notebooks** as a way of communicating with their students when necessary – for example if an unforeseen incident means people can't get into school. Class notes, homework and assistance can be given in this way.

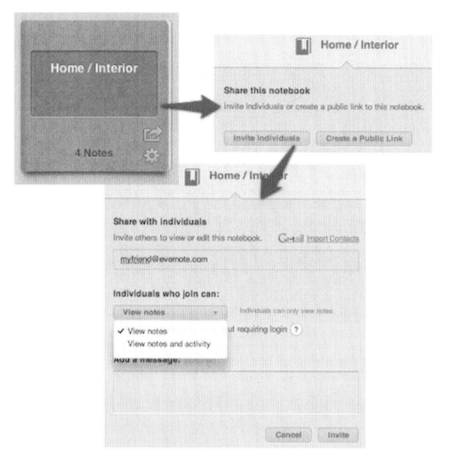

4. You can use Evernote to create employee handbooks. You can share the Notebook so that everyone in your office can access it and there are even add-on applications (such as *Skitch*) which allow you to edit and annotate these documents in ways that highlight specific, relevant information.

5. You can keep all of your important information handy – insurance information, clothes sizes, phone numbers...as you have to have a password to access your account, all this information will be kept for your eyes only and you can find it at a moment's notice.

6. Many Evernote users name their default Notebook as 'Inbox' as everything saves there – effectively making it work in a similar way to an inbox. Then, if you are particularly busy, you can save all your Notes there to start with, and organize them when you have a spare moment.

7. Another useful Notebook to have is 'Archive' which is where all the Notes go when you have finished with them. This prevents them from being deleted in case you need them at a later date, but stops them from cluttering up your 'Inbox' and other Notebooks.

8. Ink Notes can be used for you to record your signature which you can then virtually attach onto documents when need be. This means you can sign things immediately, and saves you the time of scanning in a signed document when you have the time – your work day will run a lot smoother without this annoying task slowing you down.

9. Set a Default Notebook and treat it like an online clipboard. So whenever you save anything to your Evernote, it goes to the 'Clipboard'. You can set yourself a goal to empty Clipboard at the end of the day.

10. Using the Audio Notes like a Dictaphone means you can transcribe meeting or lecture notes when you have more time, allowing you to pay more attention when you need to.

11. A Stack or Notebook of all your research can be really handy as everything you have discovered in your search will be kept in the same place. Everyone needs to do some research at one time or another and Evernote is a great way to ensure you don't forget or lose anything. If you use your Notebook Stacks in the way you would a filing cabinet, your need for office space will reduce greatly, and the extensive search features means you don't have to spend hours looking for one piece of paper. This will save you time and money! You can also create a Stack called Travel to store multiple notebooks for different trips inside.

12. You can customize your Evernote account to suit you. You can remove unnecessary items from any of the toolbars by right-clicking in the toolbar and taking things out, or by selecting *Evernote – Tools – General*. By selecting the Evernote *look* that suits you, your work will be more productive. It's also very easy to change the way you view things on Evernote:

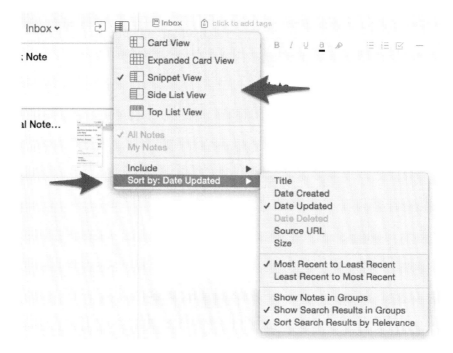

13. You can also use the audio feature to record voicemails, which means you can store them for a long time after your phone has deleted them.

14. Start keeping a diary or journal! With audio, photographs and handwritten notes available, it'll be the best kept life record you have.

15. Make Notebooks for Wish list and Dream Home. What better way to constantly remind yourself what you *want* to achieve. This constant reminder will make you more likely to follow through on your desires.

16. Evernote is a great way to keep track of your expenses. As all of your notes are kept in one place, and available on all your devices, there is no reason to forget to record something again. You can also save all of your banking information – statements, etc – so you are never too far away from your financial information.

17. If you don't want to use too many Tags, try underscore tagging. If you include the _ symbol before any tagging word, you can search your Notes easily this way.

18. If you have a premium account, these notes you share (whether it be by social media or email) can be edited by others. So you could share the shopping list with your roommates or family members and they can add to it, or remove stuff they have already purchased.

19. If you're using Evernote on a Mac system, you can actually hide your Note count by clicking *View – Sidebar Options – Hide Note Count*. Some people prefer to do this so they don't get too overwhelmed by all the information they have saved!

20. Have a 'Swipe File' for one of your Notebooks. People have been using 'Swipe Files' for a number of years, but now you can access it wherever you are! A 'Swipe File' is a collection of words and phrases that you have seen and think might be useful for yourself. You can note these down wherever you are, making sure you never forget one.

21. Naming your notes with the date is a great way to keep everything in chronological order. It'll also come in handy when referencing something later as you'll know exactly when it happened.

22. A lot of people actually use Evernote to record their haircuts. It might sound strange, but the ability to take a photo of your favorite haircut on yourself, into the hairdressers with you, mean you'll never have to suffer a terrible hairstyle again!

23. You can easily drag and drop notes or tags or even notebooks within Evernote. Dropping a document on the Evernote app icon will automatically create a new Note with the document embedded.

24. If you want to see a lot of the information associated with a Note – the Tags, the creation date, its sync status, the source URL, word count, etc – simply click the '*i*' icon on the Note and everything will show up.

25. Use the webcam to take photographs of things you need to remember; car number plates, ink cartridges, etc. That way you'll always have access to this information so you won't have to waste time hunting around for it.

26. The pictures feature can also be really handy for remembering things you like or want to try...the cover of a book, the label of a

drink, etc. Evernote also supports search of the text inside images and even handwritten notes (using OCR). You can also put *reco-Type:handwritten* or *recoType:picture* in the search box to see all your notes whose content can be extracted using OCR.

27. The pictures are also useful for saving business cards – meaning you don't have to waste time hunting for the original – your contacts will always be in one place. Business users have a comprehensive business card feature (shown later in this guide) which saves you even more time and effort.

28. Use Tags in a way which will help you locate something later. For example, 'Work' will probably be too general, but 'Project123' is more precise and much more useful. If you don't want to create too many tags, use an underscore (_) at the end of the keyword in the Note so that search function can find all the Notes that have this keyword.

29. You can use the Evernote Business account to run your entire business – colleagues can collaborate, to-do lists and even conduct a virtual meeting via editing Notes.

30. You can change the way Evernote saves the attachments to your account. Would you prefer your PDF's to be inline or as an attachment? Select *Evernote – Tools – Options – Note*, then check or uncheck the option *'Always show PDF documents as attachments'* to the method you would prefer.

31. If you have a premium Evernote account, you can replace the tired overly-familiar Powerpoint Presentation with *Presentation Mode*. This allows you to use data you already have stored in a format that you can access from any PC or MAC so there is no chance of losing it! You can make edits and turn your mouse cursor into a blue laser pointer for convenient presentation. Simply click the "Play" button above the formatting toolbar on any Note to present all Notes or limit the presentation to a series of selected Notes by highlighting the notes and then select "Start Presentation.".

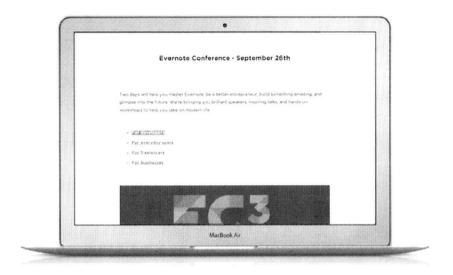

32. Use the Merge feature for your notes to prevent any clutter – just another way Evernote is helping you to streamline your information.

33. If you want some extra security for your Evernote account, you can switch to the two-step verification, meaning that your password alone won't be enough. Although you know your information is protected, it doesn't hurt to have that extra layer. All you have to do is choose *Security Summary* and click *Enable* from Evernote account settings Web page.

34. If you don't always have enough time to write everything in your To Do list, take photographs to set yourself a visual reminder.

35. If you're a premium or business user, you can actually access and edit your notes offline. If you're going to be in a lot of situations where Internet connection isn't available, this is *definitely* something to consider!

36. One of the best features of Evernote is that you can access your notes anywhere, *but* there may be some notes that you only want to keep in one place. Create a *Local Notebook* which will not be synced with your devices. Note that you won't be able to convert this into synchronized notebook later.

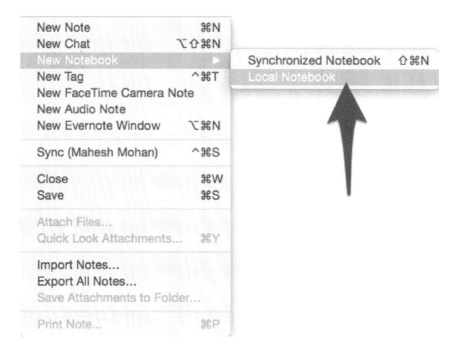

37. You can right-click any images with your notebooks to rename them or to rotate or edit it. This is just a quick way to change any necessary information or to correct any mistakes.

38. If you want to try Evernote premium before you buy it, you can do so using Evernote Points. You can earn these rewards by inviting your friends and family to try out the service. Your first 3 referrals will earn you 10 points – enough for 3 months premium and if any of your referrals upgrade, you will get an extra 5 points.

39. If you have started out with 2 or more Evernote accounts – maybe one for your personal data, another for your work documents – you can go on to merge these by exporting data from one account and importing it into another.

40. Save all your research and notes about the trip or holiday you planned into an Evernote notebook. This will be very useful for the future use to plan your next holidays or to revisit same countries.

41. If inspiration strikes at a difficult time, you can simply create a text or audio note to remind yourself of this at a better moment – useful for writers, managers, lecturers, etc.

42. Another way to use Evernote to your advantage is for telephone notes. We have all taken phone calls which have required us to write something down so that we don't forget it. Keeping these in Evernote means that however distracted we get as soon as the phone is disconnected, the information is easily revisited.

43. The Notes are a flexible feature that allows you to create information that is useful to you, so be sure to use this to your advantage by saving and storing all of this in a way that will allow you to track it with ease. The Evernote search feature is extremely comprehensive and will be discussed later in this guide.

44. Save your children's artwork by scanning those special mementos, or snapping a picture of oversized artwork with your Smartphone camera. This way you can preserve the memories of your little ones creative moments without throwing away their creations.

45. Record audio of business meetings, so that you can listen to the meeting when you need to hear it again. Mobile versions of Evernote have the ability to record Audio notes. Simply click "New Note" > "Attachment Icon" > "Microphone Icon".

46. As you have seen, you can keep all the different parts of your life separate, meaning you never get confused again. This means less of your precious time is spent organizing, and more can be spent ticking things off of your to do list!

47. Evernote is the perfect platform to convert your office or home to a 'paperless environment'. By connecting a scanner to your computer and Evernote, you are just one click away from turning clutter into an organized, searchable database with context. Use consistent titles on your scans: "123 Street – Gas Statement – January 2015" and tags to put every piece of paper at your finger tips. Sign up for e-bills and drag PDFs right into Evernote. Create filters in your email to auto forward bills to your Evernote email address to automate as much as possible. You can auto forward newsletters to your "read later" list too!

48. Have a Tag named "Ideas". It's better to use a Tag for it versus a Notebook because ideas can apply to any subject.

49. Notebooks are arranged alphabetically in the sidebar. If you want a Notebook to appear at the top of the list, use punctuation before it.

50. Finally, be sure to curate your notes as often as possible. Allowing your notes to pile up with titles that mean nothing to you and tags that are misspelled or pointless will leave you with a time consuming task later on.

ADVANCED BLACKLISTED TECHNIQUES

"No need to worry about putting it in the right notebook or attaching the right tags. This tool is perfect for capturing what's running through your head before it runs away"

So this guide has already looked at the basics of Evernote, but now is the time to get onto the more advanced features which are designed to make your life *even* easier! The first thing to look at is the **extra Note features available**, which are designed to save you time and make your life run more efficiently.

Encrypting Text

You can encrypt the text within a Note to **add an extra level of protection** to it - just in case you'd feel better with the extra security! You can use this to store sensitive data such as passwords, client details or personal information. It's worth noting that while you can do this within a Note, *you can't encrypt the entire Note or Notebook*. Encrypting the text you wish you protect is easy. All you need to do is open the required Note and highlight the text. Then you need to right-click to bring up a drop down menu.

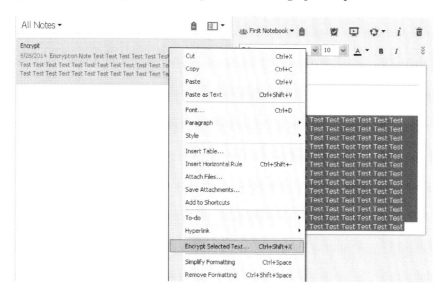

Once you have chosen '*Encrypt Selected Text...*' from the menu, a box will appear asking you to set a passphrase which will decrypt the text. Do not forget this passphrase because Evernote won't store this information anywhere.

It is a good idea to include a hint to help you remember what you have set as your passphrase.

This will the encrypt all of your text, simply showing the following symbol until you unlock it with the passphrase.

Toc For Notes

Creating a table of contents using note links is a great way to locate notes that are all linked by a single purpose for easy and quick access; which can be extremely handy for research, project notes or school work. To do this, you need to select the Notes that you wish to include in the table of contents in the list on the left-hand side of the screen. For Windows you will hold *Ctrl* and click on the relevant Notes and for Mac, you'll CMD and click.

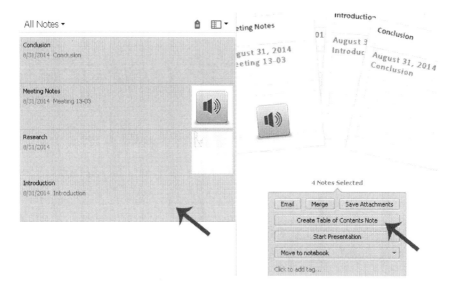

You will then produce a list of options on the right-hand side of the screen. Choose '*Create Table of Contents Note*' which will then produce a box with the message 'Synchronizing Notes'. The TOC Note will be created.

The Notes within the table of contents will be numbered and listed by their title name. Simply left-click on the Note you wish to view, and Evernote will take you right there. This can be useful for your personal organization or presentations, or even for guiding others throughout your work.

You might look at this feature and instantly think about work, but there are some other more unusual ways it has been used. These include:

- **A fitness plan** – link to programs, diets and your exercise to-do list.

- **Your library** – notes you have made on books you have read, books you want to read and when your books are due back to the library.

- **Fantasy sports league** – all the information you need about your team and your league is easily accessible with a TOC.

Geotags

Geotagging is the process of **adding geographical identification to various media**, and is available on Evernote. Your mobile device with GPS allows you to set the location where you created a Note. This can be useful for searching, recalling information and organizing your Notes; for example where you met someone, where you wrote a review or where you were when a piece of inspiration struck. You can turn this on automatically when downloading your Evernote app, or you can change it at a later date using 'Settings'.

You can later use the '*Atlas*' tab on the right-hand side of the screen to have your Notes organized by location. You can also search through your Notes by using this information, which can be very useful for business information, or even for your personal Notes.

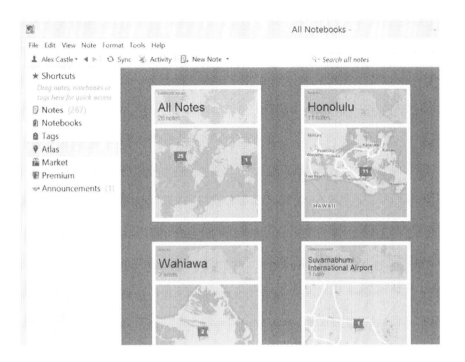

ULTIMATE TIME
SAVING TACTICS

Evernote is all about managing your time effectively, and the following techniques will all make the day-to-day running of your life much easier.

Templates

You may wish to **create a template in Evernote** to ensure the future note-taking process is much quicker and more efficient. If you use the application for the same task over and over – maybe for invoices – then this is a great idea to allow Evernote to take a lot of the hard work off your hands.

There is an add-on application which is designed specifically for this purpose, and it's called *KustomNote*. It's a simple system which **allows you to fill in and save templates to your Evernote account**, so that the information is constantly readily available to you.

To use this application, you need to go to the website http://kustomnote.com and sign up for a free account. All you need is your name, email address and a password. This will come up with a screen that allows you to connect KustomNote to your Evernote account, create your own template or browse the existing ones the app has available for public use.

The templates already available cover absolutely every possible need from doctor's appointments to homework schedules. Chances are you'll be able to find whatever you need as a starting point, but if you'd like to keep your template more personalized, it will be better for you to create your own.

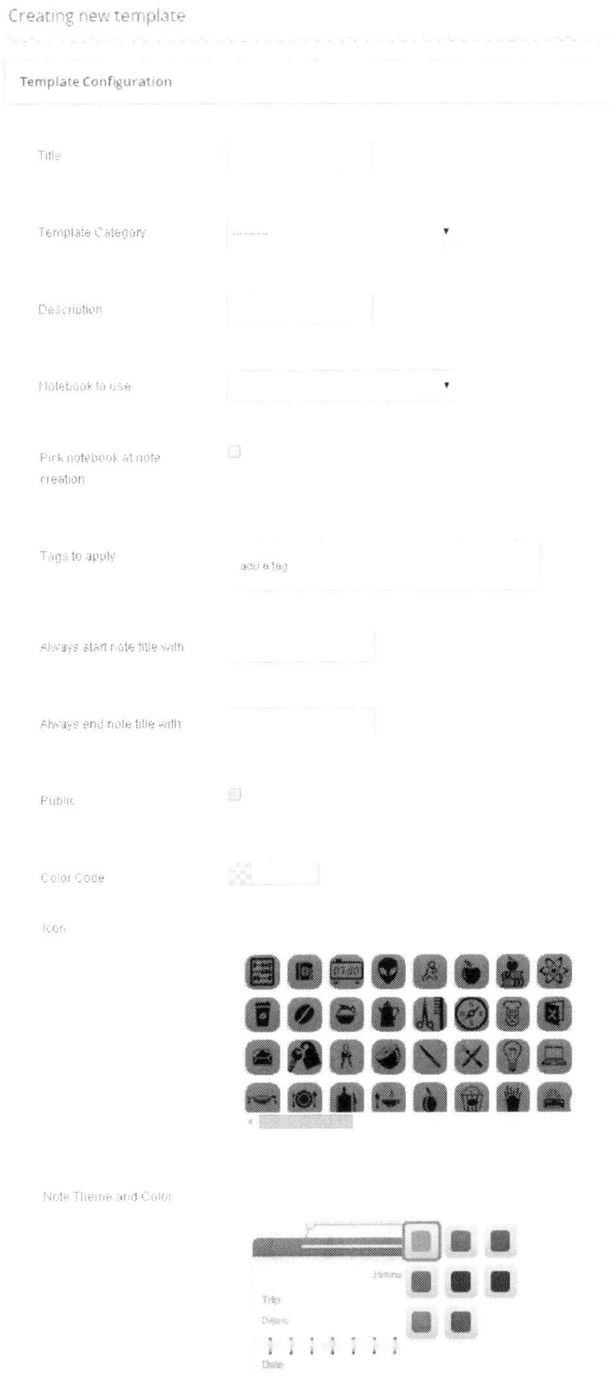

EVERNOTE

Creating new template

Template Configuration

Title

Template Category ⌄

Description

Notebook to use ⌄

Pick notebook at note creation ☐

Tags to apply
add a tag

Always start note title with

Always end note title with

Public ☐

Color Code

Icon

Note Theme and Color

The options available to create your own allow you to change everything you could want to ensure that your template works for you.

This isn't the only way you can create a template however. If your needs are much more simplistic, you can simply create the Note template you require in Evernote, then **export** this and save it to your desktop (or somewhere easily accessible). To do this, right-click on the Note you wish to export on the list on the left-hand side of the screen.

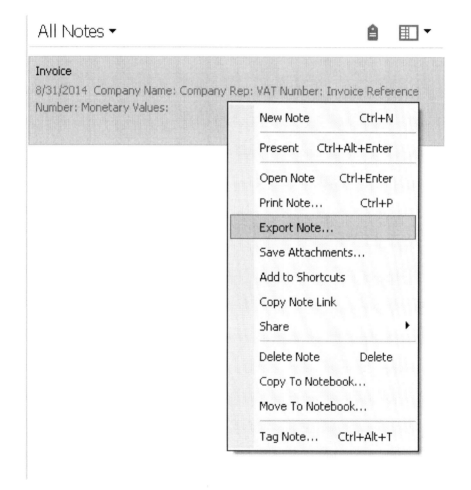

This will then provide you with a list of export options. Select the first option on the list to save it as an *.enex* – or **Evernote export** – file.

Once you have completed this action, a message will pop up in your Evernote application stating 'Export Successful!' An icon will then appear on your desktop, which you can left-click to drag and drop this onto Evernote every time you wish to use it. This will open a new Note using the same format and Tags as your template.

There is also a third way that templates can be created to make your Evernote usage easier and quicker, and that is via the *TextExpander* (bit.ly/textexpanders) apps.

These work by inserting a certain pre-set keystroke sequence, which is initiated by a hotkey combination. So for instance, you could use the text *homephone* to instantly be replaced with your home phone number, meaning you don't have to waste time looking for it if it isn't a number you remember offhand. This can also be used to remember a much more complicated set of text than that, you can set a hotkey to recall and entire Note template, making the note creation process much quicker and easier. These TextExpander apps do cost a lot of money (or are free), but are worth it if they are something you are likely to use regularly.

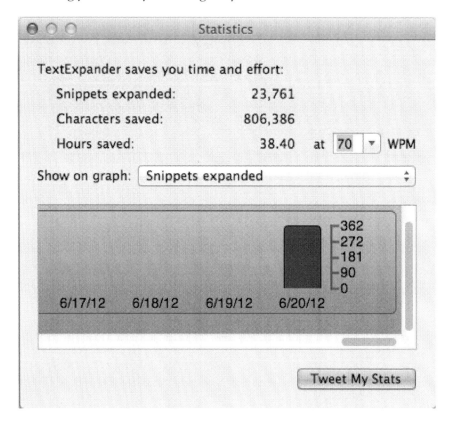

Web Clipper

The Evernote **web clipper allows you to save online content to your Evernote account for later use**. It works in a similar way to bookmarking websites, but is much more effective as you can save the actual part of the webpage you want to return to. You can also add annotations to highlight particular sections.

You can download the web clipper application from the Evernote app store, or www.evernote.com/webclipper - which offers you the download option for whatever Internet browser you use.

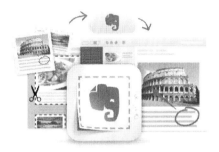

Evernote Web Clipper

Collect the best of the web, all in one place. Quickly and easily clip articles, text, and images right into Evernote.

Download for Chrome

Once you have followed the download instructions, you will be presented with the following message, letting you know that Evernote web clipper has been added as an extension to your web browser.

Evernote Web Clipper has been added to Chrome.

Use this extension by clicking on this icon.

Manage your extensions by clicking Extensions in the Tools menu.

Sign in to Chrome to get this extension, your history, and other Chrome settings on all your devices.

This means that the **Evernote web clipper logo** will appear along the address tool bar on your web browser. This is what you will click on when you have found a website you wish to 'clip'.

Once you have picked something you'd like to save to Evernote, and you have clicked on the icon, the following options will appear. You can chose the type of note you wish to label this as, the Notebook you want to send it to and if you'd like to add any Tags.

You can click on the 'Options' logo at the bottom of the dropdown menu to bring up a variety of extra options, depending on how much detail you want to include in your web clipped note. After the note has been clipped and synced, another box will appear showing related notes and the option to share your new note via social media or email.

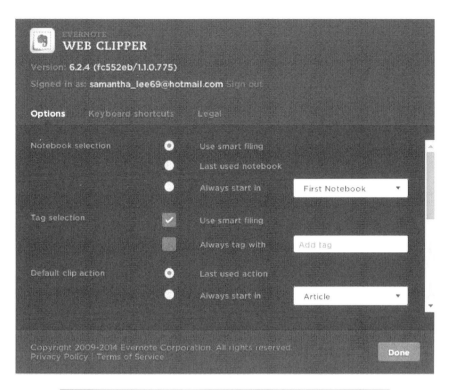

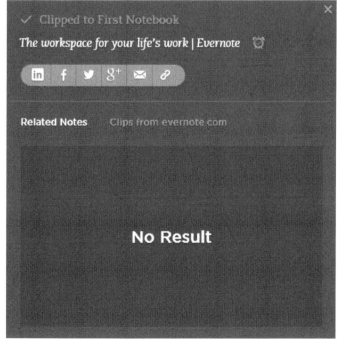

You will then be able to view this web page in Evernote where you can use all the same tools as for any other Note. You can also choose to use the **web clippers screenshot option**, by selecting '*Screenshot*' from the initial dropdown menu, which allows you to annotate the image, giving feedback or highlighting specific things you'd like to refer back to at a later date.

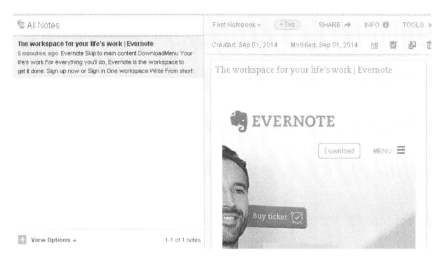

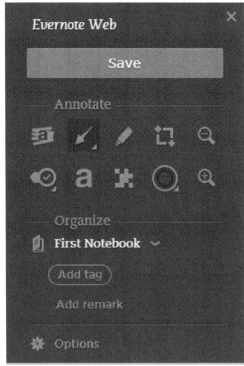

Evernote web clipper allows you to bookmark websites, but **it is much more effective than the bookmark feature** already on your web browser as it allows you to select the specific part of the web site you wanted to re-call, the note is available on any device you have the Evernote app down-loaded and you can share, annotate and edit the piece to suit your personal needs, which is ideal when you are completing research.

Reminders

Reminders allow you to manage your deadlines in a very effective way. They are very easy to set up and alert you to what you need to do with an in-app notification, an email and a badge on the app tile, so there isn't a chance of you missing an important cut-off date.

To set one up, you need to open the Note you wish to be linked to the reminder and then click on the alarm clock symbol on the top tool bar on the right-hand side of the screen. This will give you a dropdown menu of options.

To set a reminder, click '*Add Date*' which brings up a calendar, allowing you to set the required date for your personal deadline. You will also be given the option to set a time for your reminder, which is perfect for if your Note relates to a meeting. Once you have set the reminder, the Note will stay at the top of the list of Notes on the left-hand side of the screen, so you can keep an eye on what you need to achieve. As you can see, if you finish your task early you can '*Mark As Done*'.

You can use this to remind yourself of the next deadline on your to do list. To **turn your list into list with checkboxes**, simply create the list with each item on a separate line, then highlight them and left-click which will provide you with a dropdown menu. Select '*To Do*' then '*Add Checkbox*' (or use the keyboard shortcut '*Ctrl*', '*Shift*', '*C*'). You can then set a reminder when your next item is due, then check it off once it's complete.

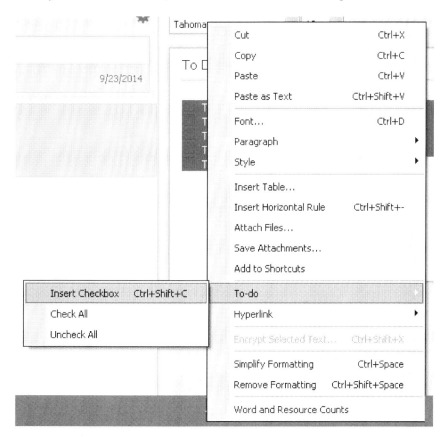

This is a fantastic way to keep on top of everything you need to do —work projects, school work or even dental appointments. With access to your To Do list, wherever you are, you'll never forget anything again!

You can also get more organized by creating a **weekly or monthly planner** using **KustomNote** at kustomnote.com (an example of available template shown below), or by creating your own. The initial moments spent organizing your schedule, will save you a lot of time in the long run as you won't be wasting minutes working out what needs to be done, or searching for the things you need to complete a task – because Evernote will have it all!

Keyboard Shortcuts

There are many keyboard shortcuts in Evernote, designed to make your usage quicker and easier. Below is a table of the most useful to get you started:

Mac Shortcut	Windows Shortcut	Evernote Function
[⌘] [n]	[Ctrl] [n]	New Note
[^] [⌘] [t]	[Ctrl] [Shift] [t]	New Tag
[Shift] [⌘] [n]	[Ctrl] [Shift] [n]	New Notebook
[^] [⌘] [s]	[F9]	Sync
[⌘] [s]	[Ctrl] [s]	Save Note
[Delete]	[Delete]	Delete Note
[Shift] [⌘] [m]	*Not Available*	Merge Notes
[Shift] [⌘] [x]	[Ctrl] [Shift] [x]	Encrypt Selected Text
[⌥] [⌘] [f]	[Ctrl] [Alt] [f]	Search Notes
[⌥] [⌘] [s]	[Ctrl] [Shift] [s]	Save Search
[⌘] [r]	[Ctrl] [Shift] [a]	Reset Search
[⌘] [f]	[Ctrl] [f]	Find Within Note...
[⌘] [g]	[Ctrl] [g]	Find Next
[Shift] [⌘] [g]	[Ctrl] [Shift] [g]	Find Previous
[⌘] [j]	[Shift] [Alt] [t]	Jump to Selection
[⌥] [⌘] [n]	[Ctrl] [Alt] [n]	New Evernote Window

[⌥] [⌘] [m]	[Alt] [F4]	Minimize Windows
[⌥] [⌘] [w]	[Ctrl] [q]	Close Windows
[⌘] [1]	[Ctrl] [F5]	List View
[⌘] [2]	[Ctrl] [F6]	Mixed View
[⌘] [3]	[Ctrl] [F7]	Thumbnail View
[Shift] [⌘] [a]	[Ctrl] [Alt] [t]	Show/Hide Unassigned Tags
[Shift] [⌘] [i]	[F8]	Show/Hide Note Information
[⌘] [t]	[Ctrl] [d]	Show Fonts
[Shift] [⌘] [c]	[Ctrl] [d]	Show Colors
[⌘] [b]	[Ctrl] [b]	Bold
[⌘] [i]	[Ctrl] [i]	Italic
[⌘] [u]	[Ctrl] [u]	Underlined
[⌘] [+]	[Ctrl] [Shift] [>]	Bigger
[⌘] [-]	[Ctrl] [/]	Smaller
[⌘] Plus [{] for Left [|] for Centre and [}] for Right	[Ctrl] Plus [l] for Left [e] for Centre And [r] for Right	Align
[Shift] [⌘] [u]	[Ctrl] [Shift] [b]	Toggle Bulleted List
[Shift] [⌘] [o]	[Ctrl] [Shift] [o]	Toggle Numbered List
[⌘] [k]	[Ctrl] [k]	Add Link

[Shift] [⌘] [k]	[Ctrl] [Shift] [F9]	Remove Link
[Shift] [⌘] [t]	[Ctrl] [Shift] [c]	Insert To Do
[Shift] [⌘] [h]	[Ctrl] [Shift] [-]	Insert Horizontal Rule
[Shift] [⌘] [f]	[Ctrl] [Space]	Simplify Formatting
[⌘] [Shift] [d] [⌘][⌥] [Shift] [a]	[Alt] [Shift] [d]	Insert Date/Time
[⌘] [x]	[Ctrl] [x]	Cut
[⌘] [c]	[Ctrl] [c]	Copy
[⌘] [v]	[Ctrl] [v]	Paste
[⌘] [z]	[Ctrl] [z]	Undo
[Shift] [⌘] [z]	[Ctrl] [y]	Redo
[⌘] [s]	[Ctrl] [s]	Save
[⌘] [a]	[Ctrl] [a]	Select All
[Shift] [⌘] [p]	[Ctrl] [F2]	Print Preview
[⌘] [p]	[Ctrl] [p]	Print
Not Available	[Ctrl] [Shift] [e]	Email
[⌘] [+]	[F7]	Spellchecker

3 SIMPLE STEPS
TO STAY CONNECTED

IMPORTING EMAILS

You can import your emails into Evernote if you'd like to set a reminder referring to them, annotate them or simply have everything in one place. You can do this by forwarding all your emails to your Evernote email address. This is created automatically when you open your account, and can be found under '*Tools*' and '*Account Info*'.

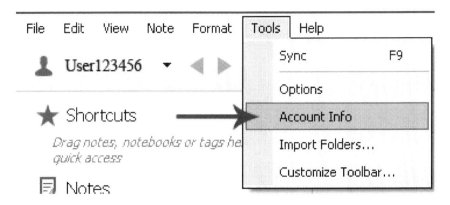

This brings up a tool box which contains **your Evernote email address**. If you send emails here, you can control which Notebook they go to by including **@** plus the Notebook's name in the subject line. You can also add a Tag by adding **#** plus the Tag after the required Notebook in the subject line.

For example: **Subject:** *@Work #Research*

A more efficient way to do this would be to have your **emails forwarded automatically at regular intervals** and an app has been designed to do this. **InQloud** does all the hard work for you, automatically creating different email addresses for each of your Notebooks and saving them to your Google contacts. All you need to do is sign up to http://inqloud.com and follow the simple instructions to set up the forwarding instructions. You can either choose to send specific emails to the right Notebooks, for instance forwarding emails that require immediate action to your 'To Do' folder, or you can have every email sent so you don't miss a thing.

You could also choose to use the web clipper to copy across email threads so you can read the entire conversation in one go. To do that, simply open the required email conversation in Gmail, before clicking on the web clipper icon, found next to your web page address bar.

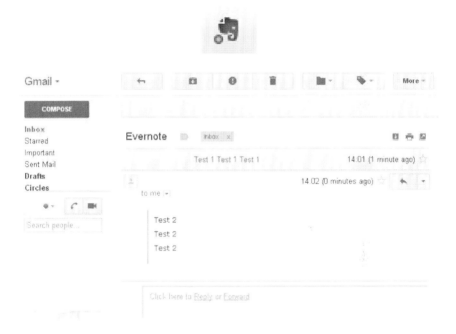

This will then bring up the following message giving you the option of what messages you want to transfer, and to what Notebook within Evernote.

Once you have selected all the options to suit you, the next time you synchronize your Evernote application, the emails will appear where you have sent them, allowing you to read through them at leisure, opening them in Gmail as you wish.

There are many ways to get your emails into Evernote; and many reasons you may wish to record your conversations in this way – to add them to your To Do list, the recall them easily when needed or even to share them via social media. Whatever you need the feature for, there is no denying that it's a useful one!

Icloud And Google Contacts

You can **sync your iCloud and Google contacts to Evernote**, ensuring data you have already stored can be transferred easily. Again, having everything in one place makes your life so much easier, and with Evernote's extensive search feature (discussed later in this guide), everything is very easy to locate.

iCloud is the only storage system devised by Apple. You can sync this to Evernote by using **GoodSync** at http://bit.ly/goodsyncwin. This app downloads to your PC or mobile device (Mac version can be found at http://bit.ly/goodsyncmac), backs up your files and **allows you to move files between applications; including iCloud and Evernote**. This way you can back up everything you need, and save them to Evernote – where you can use all of the brilliant time-saving features to manage your life effectively.

You can also **synchronize all of your Google Contacts to Evernote**, ensuring all the contact information you'll ever need will always be at your finger tips. To do this, you can use **Zapier** (zapier.com) which works in a similar way to IFTTT. Zapier has the following recipes involving Google Contacts and Evernote available, and they are extremely easy to set up.

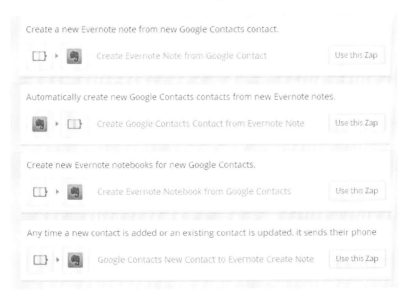

You can also import your Gmail contacts through the desktop version of Evernote by clicking on *Settings* at the top right-hand side of the page. You then choose *'Connected Services'* from the menu on the left-hand side of the screen and click *'Connect'* next to the Google logo.

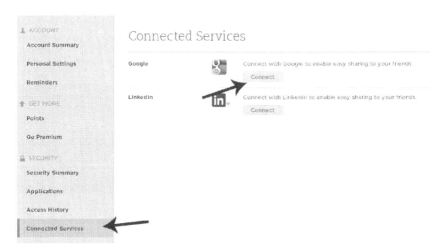

Once you have entered in your Google information, a list of options will appear. Select *'Manage your Contacts'* followed by *'Accept'* which will then ensure your accounts are connected.

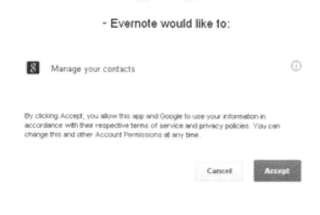

Evernote On Your Mobile

Having the Evernote application on your mobile phone means that you can access all of your information on the go! You can go over your meeting notes during the commute to work, continue your research whilst waiting for a lecture or take photograph, allowing Evernote to use the Optical Character Recognition so that your Note will be easier to find at a later date...the possibilities are endless.

You aren't restricted when it comes to using Evernote on your phone. You can still create all the different Notes – text, ink, image and audio. You can even clip web pages and search through all of your current Notes. You can also access and use your Notebooks, Stacks and Tags. In fact, there isn't a lot you can't do! It is available on iOs, Android and Window's phones, so everyone should be able to access it in this way.

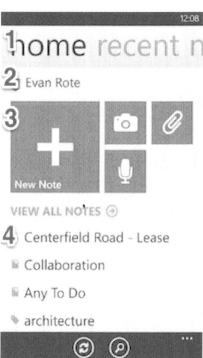

STUNNING WAYS TO REVOLIUTIONIZE YOUR LIFE WITH EVERNOTE SEARCH

*"When you start to get thousands of notes in your Evernote,
you'll find searching them quickly is more and more important"*

When you want to find something in Evernote, you don't want to waste time looking manually through all of your Notes, you want **a search bar that finds everything relevant** quickly and easily – which is exactly what Evernote has provided for you at the top right-hand side of the screen.

You can type in whatever word you want to search for and Evernote will scan through all your Notes and Tags and produce a list on the left-hand side of the screen of everything containing your search term.

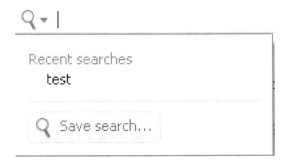

If the search term is something that you intend to use regularly, you can select '*Save Search*' from the dropdown menu which will produce the following box, allowing you to name the search and put in the query terms. You can put in multiple query terms, separated by a comma.

You can also set up a new saved search by selecting '*File*' and choosing '*New Saved Search*' from the dropdown menu. This will produce the same box as above. Your saved searches will appear the next time you click in the search box.

The downside of a search is that Evernote will find all the Notes containing *all* the words in you search, but you can get around this. One way is to change the way you use the search bar. You can use **plus** and **minus** symbols to ensure Evernote only finds what you want it to. For example *Research +Project1 –Project2* will only find Notes containing 'Research' and 'Project1'.

You can also use the term '*any:*' to ensure Evernote finds the Notes containing any of the search terms. This can be extremely useful and time saving – it prevents you from having to look for every word individually. For example *any: science test project*. This method also works when looking for a specific Notebook (*Notebook: [Notebook Name]*), Note (*Intitle: [Note Name]*) or Tag (*Tag: [Tag Name]*).

Premium and Business Evernote users can search in a more advanced way to free users. Their search also extends to documents attached to Notes making it much more advanced and useful. If you intend to use Evernote for your documents, the premium account is worth it for this feature alone.

Best Tagging Practises

As the number of Notebooks you can have is limited (this limit increases depending on the type of account you have) and each Note can only sit in one Notebook, **Tagging is a great way to organize your Notes** is a different way, and is an essential feature to the Evernote search options. You can have thousands of Tags, and multiple Tags per Note, making the organization system much more flexible and complex. *How to set a Tag* has already been discussed previously in this guide.

How you use these Tags depends on how you wish to use your account. Some people prefer to only use a few Tags with specific set of terms that they intend to look up later, others like to use a wide range of Tags to suit anything they may search.

This being the case, there are a **few things to remember about Tagging**. Tags are primarily set so that an Evernote search of a specific keyword will bring up all the Notes that contain that Tag. It's important to remember that these searches also include every word inside the Note, so you *don't need to Tag a word that is already written inside the Note's content*. It's better to set Tags that are meaningful for you, so that the Note will come up when you need it, not for every single search. The search feature is a useful one, you don't want it to become overflowing and difficult to use.

Research has shown that **most people use Tags for the following categories**: people, business names, projects, dates or keywords that relate to their own work. However you use Tags, just be sure that it's a useful feature that saves you the time of searching through your Notes manually.

The Evernote Cheat Sheet: A Quick Look Guide For Advanced Searches

A few of the advanced search options have already been discussed in this chapter, but there are many more possibilities you can use to make the search bar work even harder for you.

Search Term	Description	Example
Intitle:	As discussed, this searches within the title of the Note.	*Intitle: Work* will find all the Notes with 'Work' in the title.
Notebook:	This searches for Notes within a specific Notebook.	*Notebook: Blogging* will on find the Notes within your Blogging Notebook.
Any:	This will find any of the words in the search term (normal searches look for Notes containing *all* the words.)	*Any: Home Family Fun* will find all the Notes containing any of those three words.
Tag:	This will only search for the Notes Tagged with a specific keyword.	*Tag: Information* will find all the Notes with the Tag 'Information'.
-Tag:	This will search for Notes *not* Tagged by the search term.	*-Tag: Work* will find all the Notes that don't have the Tag 'Work'.
Created: [datetime]	This searches for Notes created on or after the set date. The date must be formatted YYYYMMDD or as a date relevant to the current date.	*Created: 20120313* will find all the Notes posted since 13th March 2013. *Created: day-2* will find Notes created up to 2 days ago.

Updated: [datetime]	This works in the same way as the 'Created: [datetime]' but only refers to the last time a Note was modified.	*Updated: week-3* will search for Notes that have been modified up to 3 weeks ago.
Resource:	This allows you to search for a specific type of Note; audio, webcam, ink, etc.	*Resource: Image/JPEG* will find all the Notes containing JPEG images.
Latitude: Longitude: Altitude:	This will search for the location where you created the Note depending on the co-ordinates you set. These all work in the same way.	*Latitude: 37* will find all the Notes created at a greater latitude than 37. *Latitude: 37- Latitude: 38* will narrow the search to between 37 and 38.
Source:	This searches for Notes according to the source that created them. This can include external application.	*Source: Mobile* *Source: Mail.smtp* *Source: Web.Clipper*
RecoType:	This looks for Notes that contain some sort of recognition information, such as an image containing text.	*RecoType: Picture* will find all Notes that have been processed by Evernote's image recognition system.
Todo:	This searches for Notes containing checkboxes. *Todo** brings back all the Notes with checkboxes, whether they are checked or not.	*Todo: True* will find all Notes containing checkboxes where one of the boxes is checked. *Todo: False* brings back all the Notes with only unchecked boxes,
Encryption	This searches for Notes containing encrypted text.	*Encryption* is all you need for this search term.

The search bar is one of the highest rated things about Evernote, and with all of these clever tricks to get it working to your advantage; it's easy to see why.

4 SECRET WAYS TO
USE IMAGE FILES

You can **incorporate your pictures to Evernote** in a range of different ways. One way is to create a new Note, then click '*File*' and '*Attach Files*'. This provides you with all of your Documents which gives you the opportunity to select the one you want. As shown previously, this method works for all files, not just pictures. You can attach everything from written documents to PDF's.

Another way to **import a lot of images all in one go** is to click on *'Tool'* and *'Import Folders'*.

This produces a box which allows you to add all the images you like by selecting the relevant folder. Once you have chosen the relevant folder and clicked 'OK', the images will immediately start importing, one per Note. This also works for all other document formats in the same way.

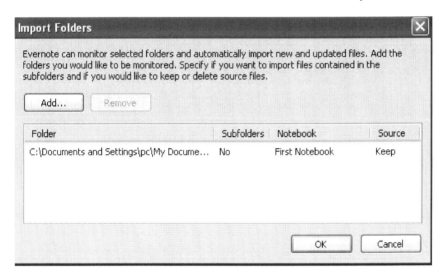

One of Evernote's best features is the fact that it can **search for text inside images using** *Optical Character Recognition (OCR)*. When you add an image to a Note, Evernote has resources that match the letters to what it recognizes as letters. This is saved to the Note in a hidden format so that it's searchable by text at a later date. This feature is available for premium and free users.

So, for example, if you were to snap a photograph of a business card (or a menu, or a wine label, etc), Evernote will recognize the shape of the letters and save that internally.

So now if you were to search one of the words (Alex, Lee, Manager, etc) using Evernote search, the Note containing this image will be shown as one of the results. This saves a lot of time spent Tagging, and hunting manually for images as you didn't title them in a useful way.

Edit PDF's

Editing PDF's is a highly sought after technique as they are often read-only with text and images, and the fact that you can do it in Evernote makes the app so much more appealing. There are many reasons you may wish to do this; you may need to give someone feedback on work they have done, you may want a certain portion of the text highlighting, whatever the reason Evernote has the answer.

Files can be attached to Notes in a simple way. By selecting '*File*' at the left-hand top corner of the screen, and choosing '*Attach Files*' from the dropdown menu.

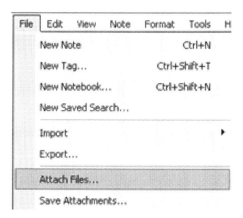

Then all you have to do is select the relevant file from the box provided and the file will attach itself to the Note. This works for PDF files, as well as spreadsheets, documents, images, etc. If you have another file which supports editing PDF's, you can then open this file and make the changes. Once you save it again, the updated version will remain in Evernote.

However, if you don't have this software currently available to you, there is an Evernote add-on called **Skitch** (evernote.com/skitch) which is perfect for this. It's a free application, which can be downloaded from the Evernote app store. It has been designed with everything visual in mind, so you can annotate images with highlighting arrows, you can edit drawings with a quick sketch or of course you can edit your PDF files to give feedback or share your ideas.

Skitch allows you to make the annotations you need to a PDF (or an image) before saving it to Evernote allowing you to open it elsewhere. A few of the current options available are arrows, highlighting, shapes, cropping and text but this list isn't extensive and updates as the app progresses.

Evernote Premium also has a PDF annotation feature, which works in a similar way to Skitch. This progresses regularly offering more and better features.

Business Cards

Snapping photos of business cards into Evernote means that you'll never lose the information of a contact ever again. Using the Evernote app on your mobile makes saving the details much easier for Evernote Business users.

When you receive a new business card, all you need to do is open the Evernote app on your phone and choose '*Camera*' to take the photograph of the card.

Once the camera opens, swipe along the options at the bottom of the screen until you reach '*Business Card*'.

Then you can take the photo, and Evernote will use optical character recognition to pick up the text and submit it to the business card form.

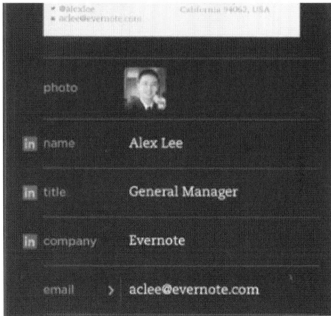

You can then check through all of this information and edit it if necessary. The form will then transfer into Evernote and all your business cards will be uniform and kept in one place.

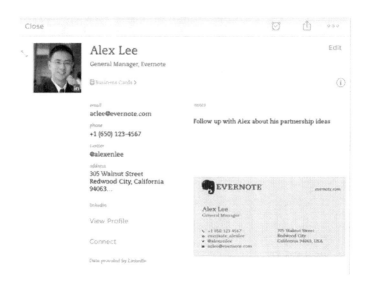

Scanning

You may wish to **scan documents into Evernote** so that you can carry them with you wherever you go. It's a great way to 'go paperless' as you'll no longer need to carry work documents around with you which makes your life much easier to manage. You will also be able to access all of these documents wherever you are, so all the information they contain will always be with you – this can be anything from your CV to your new home building plans.

There are many **scanning apps for Evernote** currently on the **market** at evernote.com/market and below is a comparison of the *top rated applications*.

CamScanner

CamScanner (www.camscanner.com) allows you to scan any documents into Evernote, quickly and easily. All you have to do is take a photo of the required document and the app then takes care of the rest for you. CamScanner allows you to scan multi page documents of any kind (including graphics, PDF's, etc) and then it crops and enhances the image for you. Then you can edit and share the image to suit your requirements.

ScannerPro

ScannerPro (readdle.com) works in a similar way to CamScanner. You take a photo of the image and then the app will send it to Evernote for you. You can batch upload with this application, then set its destination Notebook, making the entire process quick and simple.

SpeakToIt

SpeakToIt (assistant.ai) does much more than simply scanning. It acts as your virtual personal assistant; performing tasks, answering questions and alerting you to important events, so if you want an app with multiple uses, this might be the best one for you.

FastEver Snap

FastEver Snap (bit.ly/fasteversnap) takes photographs and sends them directly to your Evernote account. You can resize photos, Tag them and set a destination Notebook before sending them off. The app works quickly, but has less editing features than others.

So as you can see, each scanning app has its advantages, it all depends on which one suits your personal requirements.

MASTERING EVERNOTE RECIPES

Evernote is one of the applications which supports the **IFTTT – 'If This Then That'** building blocks. IFTTT works on a very simple premise *'If'* something happens at *'This'* it triggers a reaction, *'Then'* an action will happen at *'That'*. This means you can set one of your other social media accounts or applications to send automatic Notes to Evernote.

To do this, you need to sign up to an account at http://ifttt.com which takes only a moment. You need a username, an email address and a password. This will take you to the homepage where you will begin to set up your first recipe.

You will need to click on '*Create a Recipe*' to start and you will be guided through a simple seven step process. First you'll initiate the '***This***' which is the trigger for the event. There are many social media accounts available here. Click on the one you wish to go with (For instance Blogger) and activate the relevant account if necessary – which you will only need to do once.

Please activate the Blogger Channel.

You'll then want to click '*Continue to the next step*' which will take you a list of trigger options – these are different depending on what social media account you choose.

 Choose a Trigger   step 2 of 7

Any new post
This Trigger fires every time you publish
a new post on your Blogger blog.

New post labeled
This Trigger fires every time you publish
a new post on your Blogger blog with a
specific label.

Once you have chosen the trigger you'd like, you'll be transferred to the *'That'* part of the recipe. This is the action you want to take place once the trigger has taken place.

Choose Action Channel   step 4 of 7

Showing Channels that provide at least one Action View all Channels

evernote

Evernote

Here, as you can see, Evernote has been selected, which provides the following options:

So now a recipe has been set up that every time a new blog post is created in Blogger, a Note will immediately be created in Evernote. Just think of how much time those few moments setting up a recipe will save you in the long run, and with all the apps currently signed up to IFTTT, there isn't a lot you can't do!

These recipes can connect anything together, and are designed to make your life run much more efficiently, while saving you time. Here are **the most popular Evernote recipes** from: https://ifttt.com/recipes/hot? channel=evernote:

10 TOP EVERNOTE ADD-ONS YOU SHOULD CONSIDER

There are now many Evernote add-on applications on the **market at** www.evernote.com/market, but which ones are the most useful? Of course, this all depends on your personal usage of the app, but there are some specifically designed to make your life easier and more efficient. Below are **the ten most popular** of these:

Evernote Clearly

Evernote Clearly (evernote.com/clearly) is specifically **designed to make blog posts, articles and web pages clean and easy to read**, removing all distracting adverts without reformatting the layout of the page. You can change the colors and the fonts of websites, without even having to send them to Evernote.

When you download Evernote Clearly, an icon will appear next to your address bar (in a similar way to the web clipper button). Once you click on this button, all the distracting images and adverts disappear, making the information from the web page much easier to read.

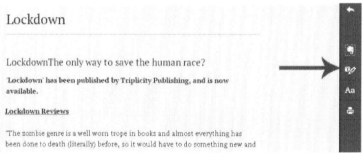

As you can see, this also gives you the opportunity to clip the information to Evernote, to highlight specific pieces of text, adjust the text size or print the cleared up version. You may need this for research or to proof read all of the text on your own website.

FileThis

FileThis (<u>filethis.com</u>) uses your online accounts for you **financial and household statements**, and delivers them **to your Evernote account** directly as soon as they become available, meaning you never miss out or forget a bill again. FileThis also allows you to access all of these accounts through one interface and password, saving you the time and effort of searching through all of your bills manually. You can even set Note reminders for when bills need to be paid – letting Evernote take out the stress of worrying about your finances.

StudyBlue

StudyBlue (appcenter.evernote.com/app/studyblue/web-apps) is designed to **convert your study materials into easy to use flash cards and practice quizzes**. This is great for revising for an exam, learning a new language or even notes for a work presentation. Chances are, all the information you'll need will be saved in Evernote anyway, and transferring these into StudyBlue is quick and easy. This means you can learn everything you need to know, at every spare moment you have – your study material will always be with you.

Postach.io

POSTACH.IO

Postach.io (postach.io) allows you to **blog from your Evernote account**, posting your selected Notes directly online. Blogging can be a great way to promote your business, projects or even just a fun side activity, and this app incorporates it into your Evernote – which you are already doing – saving you so much time and effort.

After you have signed up for your Postach.io blog, and synced it to your Evernote account, a Notebook will automatically be created. All you need to do from then on, is save the relevant Notes to that Notebook, and they'll automatically be published on your site. This means you can blog on the move, and work on blog posts for a period of time, before uploading them. With Evernote Premium, you can add Google Analytics, comments and templates to your blog, making it even more useful to you.

EasilyDo

EasilyDo (www.easilydo.com) is an Evernote add-on which is **designed to work as a virtual assistant** – completely organizing your life. It offers a wide range of features including organizing your contacts, tracking parcels, checking traffic, even birthday reminders (what it does for you, depends on what you choose in the Settings). It connects to the social media accounts you allow – including Evernote, reminding you of everything need to know.

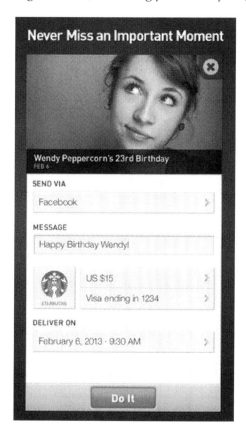

Penultimate

Penultimate (evernote.com/penultimate) is a **handwriting application for Evernote** which offers you plain, lined or squared paper. You can create much more elegant Notes with this app and it has more features available to it than the Ink notes – with more being added all the time.

Penultimate allows you to create as many Notebooks as you'd like, all of which will be synced to Evernote as a single Note. A lot of the basic Note features are also available in the Penultimate Notebooks – share, merge, delete, etc. The search feature also works in a similar way, picking out the shapes of words via OCR so you don't need to Tag each individual word.

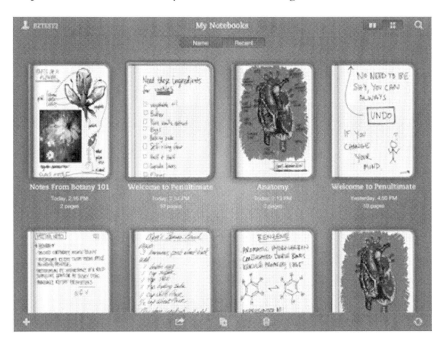

Gneo

Gneo is currently one of the hottest to-do apps, because it **focuses** more **on managing your time effectively** rather than a simple list feature. It brings your tasks and calendars together, into an ultra minimalist interface, leaving you with no distractions.

Once you have signed up for a Gneo account, and synced it to your Evernote, it will start working for you. Your To Do list will become much easier to sift through and manage, but the real magic of Gneo lies in the Forecast and Work Canvas views. The Forecast is an agenda view and it drags items from your calendar and allows you organize them according to your own needs. The Work Canvas provides you with the tasks that are most urgent for the day – allowing you to prioritize effectively.

RightSignature

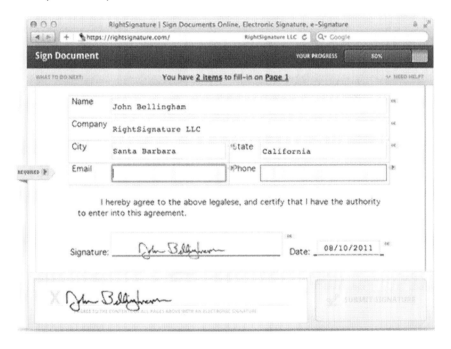

RightSignature (rightsignature.com) **turns Notes and attachments into PDFs and** from the same interface **sends them out to be signed**. As a result, a notice is sent to the recipient for a request to sign and you'll know exactly when they do.

Voice2Note

Voice2Note (<u>voice2note.dial2do.com</u>) **converts** the first 30 seconds of any of your **audio notes into text notes** which makes them more searchable. This allows you to skim through your audio notes in a similar way to your text notes, and saves you having to listen through them all to find out what you want (especially if you didn't name them particularly well at the time).

Check if the meeting is at the W hotel in San Francisco tomorrow.

This message was recorded using <u>Voice2Note</u>

ReadItLater

ReadItLater (getpocket.com/read-later-update) allows you to **copy text directly from a website** for you to read when you have more time available to you, ensuring that you don't forget something you needed to look at, or that you don't lose the information you wanted to store. This can be much handier than bookmarking web pages, because often we forget exactly what it was on a website that we wanted to return to!

50 ADVANCED TIPS
AND TRICKS

These **tips and tricks are aimed at a more advanced user of Evernote**, so if you pick the system up quickly, or have been using it for a while, these pieces of advice can help you become even more organized in your day-to-day life using Evernote.

1. Use the Evernote Tags wisely, create the following tags: ".Now", "Next", "Soon", "Someday", "Waiting", "Done". The ".Now" tag will be attached to anything that you are currently working on. The .(period) in front of the tag will force it to appear at the top of the Tag list. Find out more about this technique in the "Getting Things Done" chapter.

2. Why not save all of your recipes for your favorite meals or items from the takeaway menu to Evernote. With images, checklists and audio available, you can store detailed cooking instructions meaning that you'll never be short of something to cook.

3. You could use all of the features available to you on Evernote to research your family history. Scan in birth certificates, clip relevant web pages and conduct audio interviews with relatives – who knows what you might learn!

4. You can use your Evernote email address to subscribe to newsletters. This leaves your inbox freed up, and saves a whole load of information for you to read at a convenient time. You can also BCC your Evernote email address in to all of your correspondence, giving you the chance to look over it later. There's a Chrome plugin for Gmail called *Evernote Web Clipper* that allows users to send important emails to Evernote. The maximum number of emails that

can be sent into your Evernote email account is 50 per day (Free) or 250 per day (Premium).

5. You can track online searches, with websites, such as **Mention** (en.mention.com) and use IFTTT recipes to transport the results to Evernote. So, for example if you work in the fashion industry, you could be sure that you are constantly kept up to date with new trends.

6. If you want to utilize your time better, you can use Evernote to keep track of everything you're doing throughout the day to see how much time you're wasting procrastinating or to see if any tasks can be cut out or delegated. Set yourself a reminder every 15 to 30 minutes to record what you spent that time doing. If you would like an emailed list of Evernote reminders, you can go to *Settings* then *Reminders* and then select *Email Reminders/ Send Email Digest* to adjust when and you'd like to receive an emailed overview of your daily Evernote reminders.

7. Evernote's Hot Keys are magical. It works even if the Evernote window is not active. You have seen the keyboard shortcuts for Evernote, but did you know that you can create your own? Use the *Hot Keys* tab on the *Options* function.

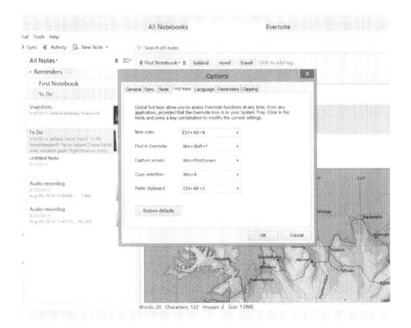

8. Travel can be made a lot easier as you can store a packing list, en-suring you don't forget anything, plus all your necessary documents. With Evernote with you constantly, you won't misplace anything you need.

9. You can create Nested Tags just like labels in Gmail. Open the Tags list in Evernote and drop a Tag over another to set the former as a sub-tag of the latter. This way you don't need to create separate notebooks for everything.

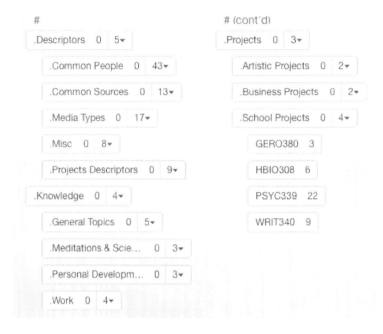

10. Try to always quit the Evernote application or close any Notes that you have open on your cell phone to avoid loss of your Note data which was stored on the other device (e.g. laptop computer) meanwhile. This is especially true if you tend to often use Evernote offline.

11. Use Note attachments rather than email attachments because it allows you to edit attachments live and save them. The files will be updated in your Note as well.

12. If you're a premium or business Evernote user, you will be able to search even when a connection isn't available, using the *'Offline Search'* function. This means that you'll be able to locate the documents you need wherever you are – even if it's so remote that there is no wifi!

13. You can turn your emails into Reminders. Compose a new message, or forward an existing one, and put an exclamation symbol in the subject line followed by the date when you would like to be reminded and send it to your Evernote address. E.g. Subject: *Pick up John ! tomorrow.*

14. Use IFTTT to send weather updates to Evernote – meaning you'll never be caught short again.

15. Don't think that Evernote can only help people working office based jobs. It can be applied to any field…even organizing an entire film shoot!

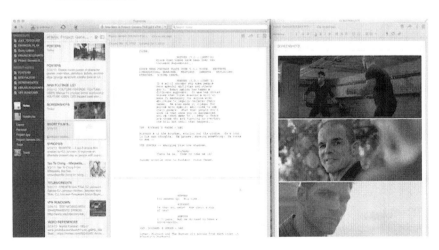

16. Scan all of your appliance manuals into Evernote. The next time something goes wrong, you won't have to spend hours looking for

the booklet to get it fixed. You can also save PDFs into Evernote by clicking "File" > "Attach File;" Drag a PDF into a Note; Drag a PDF onto the Evernote Icon; etc

17. You don't have to date your reminders; you can just set it so they appear in the small box at the top on the left-hand side of the screen. This will ensure the task is never far from your mind, but isn't necessarily scheduled.

18. Take advantage of the add-ons on offer. A lot of them are free and make Evernote so much more useful. They are specifically designed to make your life easier, so once you have found one (or more!) that suits you, be sure to use it regularly.

19. Use all of the methods to import your contacts (Google Contacts, Business Cards, etc) and Evernote will become your contact manager. You'll never lose a business contact/potential employee/your mums phone number again. There's even an option to connect the business card to LinkedIn to find even more details.

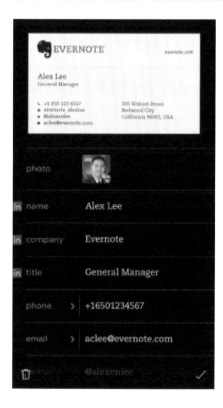

20. Your Evernote will have a 'Favorites Bar'. Drag the Notes you use regularly there to access them at a moment's notice. These shortcuts are also synced to all of your devices. Maximum number of shortcuts per account is 250.

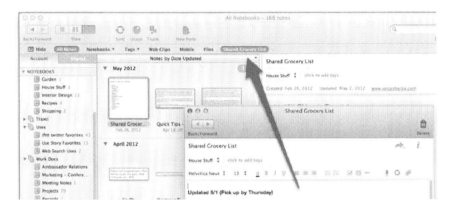

21. If you store all of your passwords to other accounts under encrypted text, make sure you pick a passphrase that you won't forget, but isn't easy to guess – particularly if some of the passwords are business or finance related! You can even search for "*Notes with encryption*" to quickly find all the encrypted notes.

22. If you want to send Tweets directly to Evernote, set up an IFTTT recipe for that. One of the IFTTT recipes can be found at ifttt.com/recipes/130933.

23. You could use the Evernote scanning feature to back up all of the documents in your office, meaning you'll never lose or accidently shred anything again. This could also work for your children's artwork. If you scan it to Evernote, you can always have it with you – and it saves cluttering up your home.

24. As there's no direct Save feature for an updated Note, try to always wait a couple of seconds before navigating out of a Note to allow some time for auto-save to complete.

25. You can access Notes history if you have Premium account. Having access to older versions of your Notes can be a lifesaver, should something critical get changed or deleted. Premium account users can access older versions of notes by logging in to Evernote on the Web, clicking the note attributes drop-down arrow for an entry, and then clicking *View note history*.

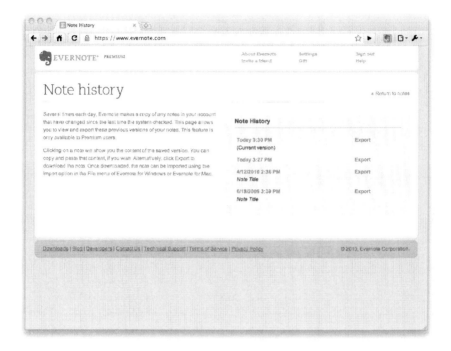

26. Use the Web clipper to save everything you have found interesting online – who knows when it'll come in handy! It also allows you attach reminders to notes, which is useful for time-sensitive pages like hotel bookings and calendar events. You can also capture things you have read on your Kindle – from ebooks, articles, etc. With the Web clipper you can decide to save just a portion of the page, the whole page, just the portion in the screen, or just the URL.

27. Use the Note links to connect all relevant Notes. Then when you perform a search at a later date, they'll create an easy read. So when doing your dissertation, link together all your research – then when you get your dream job you have all the information flowing well and easy to locate. Note links, used in a similar way to a table of contents, is also brilliant for ensuring that when you refer back to something you have created – nothing is missed! It's so easy to forget everything you make a note of, and the job of Evernote is never to forget anything so take advantage of this. Anything that is relevant, just quickly create a hyperlink then you can travel through your Notes quickly and easily.

28. Be sure to get to grips with Evernote's extensive search feature. It's

one of the best available and the more often you use it, the quicker you'll see how wonderful it is. Full list of advanced search operators can be found in the chapter above. If you don't have time to organize everything using the Tags and Notebooks feature, you actually don't have to! A lot of people aren't that organized in everyday life so struggle to do that – *but* the extensive Evernote search feature means that you can still locate those necessary files no matter what. Evernote really does work around you!

29. Use Evernote to create a whole library of stock images – you never know when you're going to need them!

30. Some people prefer to minimize the Evernote's user interface, which is easily done by switching off the functions that you don't use – maybe maps, related notes, atlas, etc.

Keyboard shortcuts	View page in Clearly	Shift + Command + Right Arrow	To change, place cursor in field and
	Clip to Evernote	Shift + Command + Up Arrow	strike key combination on your keyboard
	Highlight	Shift + Command + H	

Tags	○ Tag with		Tags to apply, when you Clip to Evernote.
	● Don't tag		

Notebook	● Use this Notebook	Read Later ‡	Notebook to clip to, when you Clip to Evernote.
	○ Use Default Notebook		

Smart Filing	○ Enable Smart Filing		Let Evernote determine what
	○ Enable Smart Filing, but just for Notebboks		Notebook clips should go into, and what Tags they should get
	○ Enable Smart Filing, but just for Tags		
	● Disable Smart Filing		

Related Notes	○ Enable Related Notes		Let Evernote fetch clips from your
	○ Enable Related Notes, but only show at bottom		account that might be relevant to what you are reading now.
	● Disable Related Notes		

31. Don't forget that a note can only exist in one notebook, but it can contain numerous tags. The tag feature will eventually become the most useful feature for searching, so it's best to start your Evernote usage with that in mind to save yourself time later on.

32. From what has been discussed in this book, you have probably figured out that you can track all of your financial documents using Evernote. Don't forget you could also keep a record of your medical information – prescriptions, appointments, that sort of thing.

33. You can use the drag and drop technique to save images, MP3s, PDF files and other presentations to your Evernote account quickly and easily. If you're dropping a Folder then Evernote will save the contents of that Folder as a Zipped file (*but do remember Note Limits*). *Tip for Mac*: You can simply drag a file/folder and drop on to Evernote's OS X Dock icon and it's saved immediately.

34. The mobile phone Evernote app has quick action buttons to save you time, so use these when you're in a rush to get straight to the note type you want!

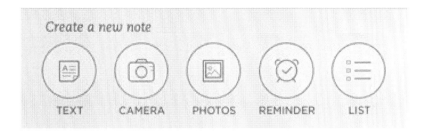

35. If you're trying to get a new job, one of your Shared Notebooks can be your portfolio! That's a quick and easy way to demonstrate all of your skills – especially if a chance encounter that has the potential to be life changing arises!

36. You can easily create script to save a Note that you use a lot to your desktop. The screenshot below shows you how to do so if you're using a Mac computer. Save the .scpt file to your desktop and double click it whenever you want the Note opened.

```
tell application id "com.evernote.Evernote"

    --- Replace NotebookName with your Evernote Notebook
    set notebookName to "NotebookName"

    --- Replace NoteTitle with the title of your note
    set matchingNotes to find notes ("intitle:NoteTitle")
    set matchingNote to item 1 of matchingNotes

    open note window with matchingNote
    activate

end tell
```

37. Many Evernote related blogs recommend adding check boxes to *any* lists you create as it gives you the satisfaction of checking tasks off once you've completed them – and we all know how much we like to do that!

38. You can actually apply a Tag to numerous Notes all in one go. All you have to do is Tag one Note, then highlight all the associated Notes and drag them to the appropriate Tag in your Evernote list of Tags.

39. Automatically create new Notes from Google Calendar events using IFTTT recipes. Each time you create a new event in your Google calendar, a new Evernote Note will automatically be created for you with all the details from Google calendar including location, description, title, start and end times.

40. One of the newest features Evernote has added is the ability to include Evernote updates in your iOs notifications. To set this up, go to iOs Settings, Control Centre and enable '*Access on Lock Screen*' for Evernote.

41. It is suggested to have fewer Notebooks, but don't forget about Stacking. Go heavier on tags and really heavy on keywords in note titles instead!

42. For recurring notes, make a "Templates" folder. Make notes templated however you like. When it comes time to use one of the templates, just go to your Templates Notebook, right click on the desired templates note, and select "*Copy note to Notebook*". Choose the notebook you'd like and you're all set. The template notes can even include tags!

43. Use Evernote with Getting Things Done (GTD) system to maximize your personal productivity. This system is described later in this

guide.

44. Save time by using Saved Searches. Enter your search term in the search bar and do a search. Once your search results are returned, go up to the menu bar in Evernote. Select *Edit > Find > Save Search*.

45. Use Evernote Capture Screenshots feature to capture information on your screen instantly. Set your Hot Keys and use Evernote's screen capture for all things Screenshot. Press the relevant Hot Key to capture a screenshot and then you will be able to capture the portion of the screen using your mouse pointer. When you release your mouse pointer the captured portion of the screen is automatically saved in your Evernote account. If you want to capture the entire screen then press the Hot Key to "Capture screen" and click anywhere on the screen once. The entire screen will be saved to your Evernote account and if you press Shift key while clicking then the screenshot will be saved in your local disk (and not to your Evernote account).

46. You can merge notes together to consolidate the information you've gathered inside your notebooks and make sure you stay at the top of the clutter in your account. The Merge option appears as soon as you select more than one Note.

47. Want to chat with your colleagues or team mates directly from Evernote? Yes, it's now possible with Work Chat. Just navigate to the Work Chat sidebar option and "Start Chatting". You can initiate a chat with any Evernote user by entering their email id.

Collaborate with Work Chat

Chat about things you're working on. Get feedback on
projects without leaving your workspace.

Start Chatting

48. It is possible that you will find two copies of the same note in
    Evernote when there is a conflict. It can happen when you edit a
    note from two devices before it was synced. In such instances,
    Evernote will place the Note in a temporary Notebook called
    "Conflicting Changes" so that you can review both versions and
    delete the one that is not up-to-date. When you are done then you
    can delete the "Conflicting Changes" Notebook itself (but it will
    appear again when there is another conflict).

49. When you click the Evernote system tray icon on Windows, it just
    opens Evernote or you can customize Evernote Icon Action to
    make it perform something else (right-click the tray icon and you
    will get it). On Mac, when you click the Evernote Menu icon it
    opens a *Quick Note*. It's a clipboard where you can save things tem-
    porarily. You can either save them to your Evernote account man-
    ually or can delete it instantly without saving. Once again, when
    you take screenshots or capture your screen on Mac OS X, it saves
    the clips to Quick Note. So, you have to save them manually or
    they'll get lost if you shutdown the computer.

50. And finally, search Evernote when you search Google! More often than not, you'll be researching something you have already looked up previously. Now you can set up Simultaneous Searches on Google Chrome Extensions to save you repeating tasks ever again:

Use Simultaneous Search: ☑

When enabled, your Google searches will also be performed on your Evernote account. The extension badge will be updated with a count of matching notes.

GLOSSARY OF
EVERNOTE TERMS

Account - You will sign up for an account with Evernote. This will be your personal workspace for all your Notes. You can have a free, premium or business account depending on your needs.

Add-on - There are many 'add-on' applications that have been developed to make Evernote even more useful. Add-ons were discussed previously in <u>10 Top Evernote Add-Ons You Should Consider</u> chapter.

Annotate - You can edit images, PDF's and documents by adding arrows, texts and other annotations.

API - "*Application Planning Interface*" – this refers to the way the software and services communicate with one another.

App Centre - This contains all the applications that you can download to incorporate with your Evernote account, according to your requirements.

Archive - You may wish to store your old Notes in an archive folder so they are out of your organized system, but can be referred back to if necessary.

Attribute - Features associated with your Note (time, date, etc).

Audio - You can attach sound to your Notes by choosing to create a '*New Audio Note*'.

Business Card - Evernote Business users can create searchable test business cards using the optical character recognition.

Client - Any application that interacts with Evernote is referred to as a 'Client'.

Clip - Content grabbed from another website/source.

Delete - You can get rid of Notes or Notebooks you no longer need, freeing up space in your Evernote account.

Encrypt - Evernote can hide certain text to add another level of security. This data can only been seen by accessing it with a passcode.

Geotag - This is the method which Evernote uses to detect and record your location on a Note.

Gmail - Google Email is very useful for Evernote as it syncs its data easily.

IFTTT - *If This Then That* allows you to create recipes which directly send data to your Evernote account.

Ink - Handwritten or drawn Notes can be created by opening a '*New Ink Note*'.

Image Recognition - Evernote processes all images and attempts to make any text visible and searchable through optical character recognition.

Import - This is the process Evernote uses to bring data into your account from your desktop files.

Keyboard Shortcut - This allows you to control Evernote from your keyboard.

Merge - You can combine your Notes, turning multiple Notes into one, which means you can collaborate on projects with colleagues.

Note - A single item stored in Evernote.

Note Link - Each Note has its own URL which you can find by using the '*Share*' options.

Notebook - A folder of stored Notes.

Optical Character Recognition - This is the process that Evernote uses to detect text within an image. This helps you to search for the image later.

Reminder - You can set a notification to remind you when you need to look at a Note.

Resource - This refers to any non-textual data stored within Evernote.

Saved Search - You can save a search that you do regularly.

Scanning - You can use scanner applications and your phone camera to scan things to Evernote.

Screenshot - You can take a screenshot of a webpage or your work, etc by using the '*New Screenshot Note*'. You will be given a vertical and horizontal line across the screen which you put in the centre of what you want to copy before left-clicking.

Search - You can search your Notes via the search bar. Unless you apply any of the advanced search techniques, it will find all the Notes containing your search term.

Share - You can share Notes or Notebooks via email or social media.

Stack - A collection of Notebooks.

Synchronization - The process of updating Evernote on your devices so *all* your content is included, regardless of where it's saved.

Tag - A meaningful description of your Note that can be used for searching.

Templates - You can create Evernote Note templates, or use an add-on to do the hard work for you.

TOC - A table of contents can be created, using links to all the included Notes in a Notebook.

Webcam - You can use your computers webcam to snap a photo to include in Evernote.

Web Clipper - The Evernote web clipper allows you to save web pages and information to your Evernote account.

MASTER YOUR LIFE
WITH EVERNOTE

The Issue

As soon as we are old enough to do things for ourselves, **we are given** small **tasks to complete**; *"tidy up your toys", "make your bed", "share with your siblings"*. The older we get, the more tasks we are given. At first its school work, then its social engagements, and eventually you'll go on to forge a career. As all of this grows, so does your to-do list, so **how do you keep organized?**

We all currently have a way of doing this, whether it's a written list, post-it notes, your email inbox, or – more likely – a combination of these. The problem with this is, **it isn't all in one place!**

The Solution

The Secret Weapon (thesecretweapon.org) has done a lot of research into this, and discovered the **features** people considered **most important for an organizational system**:

1. Keep everything in one system.

2. Allow things to be grouped separately – priority, location, project, etc.

3. Assistance in taking control of emails (hopefully bringing them down to zero!)

4. Accessible anywhere, at any time.

5.   Allow you to approach things from a different point of view, and to organize these points accordingly.

6.   Have a way to capture ALL of your ideas, saving them somewhere so you don't need to keep them in your head.

7.   Keep you in control so you don't get overwhelmed when you have a ton of stuff to do.

"Getting Things Done"

The '**Getting Things Done**' (GTD) philosophy, originally described in the novel with the same name by author *David Allen*, is a **system for getting organized and staying productive**. The idea behind it is that you spend less time doing the things you have to do, and more on doing what you want to do – and that's what everyone wants isn't it?

The process for GTD rests on the idea of moving planned projects out of your mind, and instead recording and focusing on actionable workable tasks. This allows you to complete a project in stages, without stressing over the ultimate end goal. Usually the pressure of the end result gets in the way of productivity and GTD aims to get rid of that hurdle.

In short, the GTD system is all about getting ideas out of your head so that things don't get forgotten and you don't have the stress of missed deadlines and disorganization as background noise in your brain, preventing your current productivity. It works on the premise that if you can **transfer all of your to-do's onto a system you trust**, then you will be calmer, more focused, a more capable human being.

To start the process of getting organized, the author David Allen suggests that you:

1. Identify *everything* in your life that isn't in the right place.

2. Get rid of stuff that isn't yours, or that you don't need right away.

3. Create a place that you trust and supports your working style and values.

4. Consistently put your stuff in the right place, using your new trusted system.

5. Do your stuff in a way that honors your time, energy and working style.

6. Review all of this weekly.

Evernote is set up for this methodology *exactly*. The five following steps to GTD will also demonstrate how Evernote can assist you with this GTD method. These show the way that David Allen suggests you go about all of your future projects.

Capture – this means to **note down absolutely everything relevant to the task** at hand. This is easy with Evernote; you already have all the tools to do this: Scanner, Web clipper, Check list capabilities, Audio, etc.

So for example, if your main aim is to write a novel, the capture stage would be to complete all the relevant research for this. You could use Evernote to store photographs for inspiration, relevant historical texts and even links to help you create the perfect character names.

Clarify – **break the entire project down into manageable steps**. This helps you get some things done immediately and work out what can be delegated, already freeing up more time for you.

So taking the novel idea, you could set up check lists of all the tasks you need to do – all linking to the relevant Notes with the right research or even contact details.

Organize – **create lists according to priority**. Tags, note links and notebook stacks can come in handy here to ensure everything is where it needs to be.

So once your check lists are organized, you could prioritize. For example, creating a plot line and character backgrounds will probably be your first step. An external app, such as Gneo, could work alongside Evernote to help you with this.

Reflect – take some time to **look over your to do list**. This will give you the chance to check if anything isn't quite clarified enough or if anything needs to be reorganized. It is a good idea to repeat this step throughout the process, just to check everything is going according to plan.

Engage – this is where you **get to work**. By this point, your work chunks should be manageable with everything you need already there so it should be much easier to get on with! Of course, Evernote never forgets so you don't have to worry of losing work you have already completed in the earlier stages of this process.

The initial work you put into this process will pay off in the long run. The manageable chunks of a project will make more time for what you want to do in life and can be applied to anything; from exam revision to setting up a business.

So Why Evernote?

Evernote has all the tools available to work with the GTD system; accessibility, shortcuts, an amazing search function, a selection of ways to collate your information, the ability to help you with your emails, etc, which **The Secret Weapon** goes into great detail about, and has been highly recommended by many business professionals. They have all said that combining the GTD system with Evernote has saved them loads of time and helped run their businesses more effectively.

Evernote is often referred to as '*the superhuman memory*' for the following reasons:

1. It works on both Windows and Mac.

2. It has mobile device versions, including iPhone, Android, Palm, Windows Mobile, Blackberry, iPad, and even iPod Touch.

3. It gives each user a remote cloud-based version, for syncing between device/computers.

4. It's completely free (even your online account part).

5. It has a Shared section, so groups of people can assign and share tasks/notes.

6. It has a built-in keyboard shortcut that allows you to quickly add a new task/note, regardless of what application you are in.

7. One of Evernote's best attributes: a quick method for quickly turning PC-based Outlook or Apple Mail email into a new task/note (this feature alone with transform your life).

The solution provided by The Secret Weapon goes on to suggest that you need to **create 3 Notebooks** titled *Cabinet* (this will contain all of your documents that need no action – registration documents, price sheets, medical information, etc), *Action Pending* (every Note that requires you to do something) and *Completed* (for everything you have finished). This simple system will be easy for you to follow, and will ensure that you get organized quickly. You can put *Action Pending* and *Completed* notebooks under one Stack called *Tasks*.

TIP: You can create separate Notebooks for sharing Notes with others and call a stack for them as *Shared Notebooks* so you keep all shareable Notes in one place.

Secret TIP: Create a Notebook called *Inbox* – to put all the Notes that need to be processed later. It will correspond to the physical Inbox.

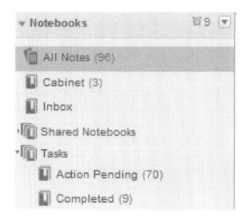

The next thing for you to focus on is **the Tags you use**. Tags are one of the main reasons why this system is so powerful. These Tags help you organize your Notes within your Notebooks in a way that is completely personal to you. I found the use of Tags as the most efficient way to organize my Notes and To-Do lists. Mainly for the reason that you can assign multiple Tags for the same Note making it extremely easy to organize and find it whenever you need. Although your requirements will be unique – after all, everyone will use Evernote for different reasons in different ways – there is a general system that can be applied to all, starting with these '*Header Tags*':

.What

.When

.Where

.Who

These will cover an aspect that you will want to categorize **every** Note in. They are then separated further by **sub-headings**:

.What

.Active_Projects

.Inactive_Projects

Ideas

Finances

Health

Relations

Emotions/Spiritual Life

Read/Review

Plus any other tags that are meaningful to you!

.When

!Daily – To be executed on daily basis (useful for forming new habbits)

1-Now - To be executed Immediately

2-Next – To be executed Next

3-Soon

4-Later

5-Someday

6-Waiting – Waiting for someone's response

.Where

@Home

@Work

@Town

.Who

[family member]

[co-worker]

[friend]

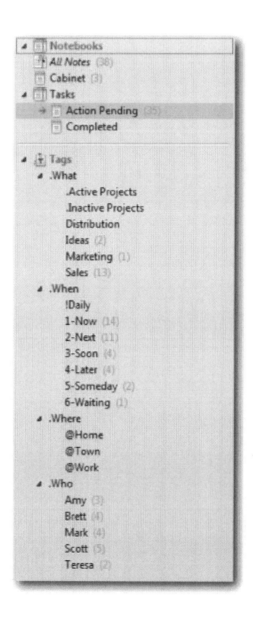

TIP: An easy way to create these Tags is simply creating a Note called Temp or something and start adding the Tags to this Note by clicking on *"click to add Tag"* field. Type each of Tags described above and press a Tab key. This will simultaneously add a permanent tag to the tag column on the left. Now you can organize the Tags by nesting them under the Headers which they belong to. You can then delete the Temp Note you created and all of the Tags will remain.

Master Tip: The Header Tags (who, where, what, when) are denoted by placing a .(period) in front of each one. This will make them to appear on the top of the Tag list. For consistency name each Notes as init-cap (start with the capital letter).

By using these minimal, but meaningful categories of Tags, **nothing will get lost** and **things can be easily found using the Evernote extensive search feature**. You can create all of these Tags in advance, then add them to Notes as required. You can even drag a collection of Notes into a Tag after they have already been created, using Nested Tags.

By the way, you can nest these as deep as you want, though I would be careful not to make your system too complex. This is often a matter of trial and error.

Convert Your Data

Once you have started to use Evernote, you will want to transfer all of your existing information into it to ensure that it's a useful application. The first thing it tells you to do is **empty your inbox**. Decide if each item needs to be deleted, archived or moved to Evernote. Don't forget to Tag each email so you know what needs doing with it. You can forward all your emails to your Evernote email address quickly and easily. Check out the <u>Importing Emails</u> chapter of this book, to remind you how to do this in the most efficient way possible.

To process the emails from your Inbox you need to move them into Evernote as one of the following items:

- **Action item** (*Action Pending* with relevant *.When* Tag) which has an associated To-do task.

- **Waiting for item** (*Action Pending* with *.When - 6-Waiting* Tag) – an item waiting for a reply back from someone.

- **Read/Review item** (*Action Pending* with *.What – Read/Review* Tag) – you want to look at this later or read on when you get time.

- **Sticky/Archive item** (This can be moved into *Cabinet* Notebook) – emails that you want around or archived for some reason (holds some idea or concept you want to remember)

Once everything has been transported and your email inbox is empty, it's time to check that all the emails have the right Tags so nothing gets missed. If things need to be actioned right away, be sure to use the relevant Tag (**1-Now**). Every email transferred into Note must have at least a **.When** tag associated to it to identify when you want this task to be done. You can then add **.What** tag to assign a project or role it belongs to, a **.Who** tag – who is it for and **.Where** you need to have it done.

Time contexts is a way of denoting relative importance and priority; in other words, what gets done first, second, etc., and the **2-Next** group of notes are those teed up to go to **1-Now** next.

Some people do find this difficult – after all, they have relied on their inbox forever – but as soon as you get to grips with it, you'll realize just how much better this system is!

TIP: If you have emails older than this year, you can move them into an Archive folder. You can process the newest emails, have your Inbox empty and process the older emails from the Archive folder.

Once you are done with importing your emails into Evernote, you can then proceed to moving all of your tasks from paper to-do lists or any other places you keep them in. Add them to appropriate context, i.e. Tags.

Usage

Now is the time to reap the benefits for all your work getting everything into Evernote. Below is a guide **how to use Evernote in the most effective way**. When it comes to mastering your life and getting organized, this is the way with the most proven success.

Daily

Every day, The Secret Weapon suggests that you follow these steps to keep on top of things:

- **Collect** – use the system described above to move any new emails or hand-written notes into your Evernote account. Of course, this won't take as long as the first time! The key here is to get them out of your head as quickly as possible.

- **Process** – add Tags to the collected items (at least .When tag) and process all of your information to confirm everything that needs doing.

- **Execute** - complete all of your !Daily and 1-Now tasks first, keeping your priorities straight. Then go over all of your 2-Next pending actions. Eventually you will get into a suitable system for you in which all of this comes very natural. As you go, think of .Who and .Where tags and update where necessary. !Daily should be the first Tag to be reviewed each morning to get going on the right foot!

- **Move it** – once you have completed any action, be sure to move it to the **Completed** notebook so that no task gets repeated unnecessarily. You can also delete the Note if you don't think you'll ever need a record about it.

- **Review** – this is a very important section, where you check over everything you have done, and see if any of the Tags relating to .When need changing. Decide which of the 2-Next items should graduate to the 1-Now pile.

Weekly

It is strongly advised to review everything on your system with **Action Pending** (from *1-Now* to *5-Someday*) on a weekly basis. This will give you a chance to reflect on everything – deadlines, priorities and even the tasks you're working on. This is extremely important as while you're working, you aren't focused on the bigger picture of your goals. This can help you do that.

So, as you can see, Evernote is perfect for this system – **Collect, Process, Execute, Review, Repeat**. People who have applied this system to their usage of Evernote have said that they wouldn't look back. They find themselves to be more organized, more reliable and calmer because they are on top of things. Who wouldn't want that for themselves?

6 BONUS IDEAS FOR EVERNOTE USAGE

As shown through this guide, Evernote is brilliant for managing your time and organizing your life. Its features are engineered towards making everything easier and run more efficiently. Listed below are **the most common ways Evernote is used**.

Research

Evernote is absolutely amazing at conducting research – whether that be for coursework or information on a new client, it has all the tools necessary, whilst keeping everything organized and in one place. You can record lectures or meetings using the audio notes, clip web pages, photograph white boards and even create a notebook which you can work on with others – conferring your notes. The checklist and reminders will also always keep you on top of deadlines meaning you never submit anything late.

Writing

A lot of extra work goes into writing a book or a paper and Evernote can help you with that. Not only can you store all of your research, but you can access it everywhere which means if inspiration strikes at an odd time, it doesn't matter, you can make a note of it. Not only can you plan your piece in Evernote, you can write it too. With such a large storage system, you can get your book written in chapters, before merging it to create the finished piece.

Business

Evernote can be the tool that helps your entire business 'go paperless'. You can keep all of your client, account and financial information in one place, encrypting all of the sensitive information. If you chose an Evernote Business account, you will have added security levels on top of this. Networking is also a much simpler; quicker task too as Evernote takes all the hassle out of this: capture information from business cards, add details from LinkedIn, etc. Email logs can also be stored, allowing the HR team to have a constant record of all the communication.

School

Evernote allows you to have portable notebooks to take into school with you – meaning none of your work or research will ever be misplaced. The To Do check lists you create mean that your coursework will always be on time. You can scan in every handout and syllabus; take pictures of the notes from whiteboard and record audio lectures. Teachers can also use Evernote to plan classes, keep track of student information and collaborate on projects with other staff members.

Finances

Evernote is a great way to keep track of your spending by scanning in receipts, which is useful when living on a budget, or just trying to keep stock of everything for the end of the financial year. Add-ons such as FileThis also ensure every bank statement and bill is automatically forwarded to my Evernote account so I can keep on top of my spending and bill due dates.

Home/Work

Using Notebooks, Stacks and Tags it is easy to keep your home and work life separate. Although Evernote is a great way to bring work home with you, by using the GTD system, you shouldn't have to, as your time will be organized accordingly!

However you do decide to use Evernote, just remember that it never forgets, so it's absolutely fantastic for keeping a record of everything that is important to you!

FAQ – GET YOUR QUESTIONS ANSWERED

Here are some of the most frequently asked questions when it comes to Evernote:

1. How do you make your important folders to rise to the top of the list?

When you title your important folders, be sure to put quote marks on either side of the word to ensure that they stay at the top of your Evernote list, grabbing your attention quickly. For example "Inbox".

2. How do you move multiple Notes?

Evernote has a multi-select feature which allows you to move multiple Notes, making the process much quicker and more efficient. As you select the Notes you wish to move, hold down '*Ctrl*' on Windows or '*CMD*' on a MAC device. You can then drag these to their new location. Alternatively, you can choose to merge, email or delete these multiple Notes with one easy click.

3. How do you send emails to your Evernote account?

You may wish to email files to your Evernote account if you are using a device that doesn't have your Evernote account downloaded. This is simple to do. You will automatically have an email address assigned to your account, which will be displayed in the *Account Settings*, under *Account Summary*. It will be something like user12345.678910@m.evernote.com.

4. How do you send emails from your Evernote account?

To send a Note or Notebook via email, you need to select the information you wish to send, and use the '*Share*' button from the top menu bar and pick '*Email*' from the dropdown menu. If you have a Gmail account, you can download your contacts to Evernote, meaning you don't even need to spend the time typing in the individual email addresses.

5. How do you use Evernote to post to FB, Twitter, LinkedIn?

To share Notes or Notebooks via your social media, you need to select the information you wish to share, and use the '*Share*' button from the top menu bar. 'Facebook', 'Twitter' and 'LinkedIn' will appear as sharing options in the dropdown menu. If you're already logged in to the relevant social media account, the sharing process will be even quicker.

6. How do you use note links to reference other notes?

This is a great technique that can help you reference other Notes within the Note you're working on – so for instance if you're collaborating on a project or planning a trip, you can link to other parts of the process. To do this, you simply right-click on the Note you wish to link to, and chose '*Copy Note Link*' from the dropdown menu. Then on the Note you wish to include the link, right-click and chose '*Paste*'. It will appear as a hyperlink.

7. How do you use special keywords for email?

You can use your Evernote email address to specify a destination for the information. To send the data to a Notebook include the @ symbol followed by the name of the Notebook in the subject line. You can also include the # symbol with the required existing Tag too. Just remember, if you're including both, do the Notebook name first.

For example: *Subject: @Work Project 1 #Urgent.*

8. How do you organize your Notebooks and Tags for maximum efficiency?

Most people will want to organize Evernote as much as possible, to save time searching through for important information later on. The best way to sort Notebooks is into Stacks. These can be something as simple as '*Work*', '*Personal*' and '*Finance*' with the more specific organization within each Stack. The key to consider with Tags is less is more. Evernote records each word within the Note, so a Tag is unnecessary unless it isn't an included word. Also, be sure that it's a meaningful tag such as '*Urgent*' or '*To_Do*'. If you aren't going to use it at a later date, it's a waste of time setting it as a Tag.

9. How do you create super-fast shortcuts to special notes?

Adding '++' to the Tag will mean that it rise to the top of your Tag list and you can find the Note quickly and easily.

10. How do you use Evernote as file storage facilitator?

You can scan in all of your images and documents and keep them in Evernote as a filing system, freeing up your need for the paper copies. The search feature makes it all much easier for you to find what you need quickly and easily.

11. What are the best Tagging practices?

Your Tags will obviously be there to suit your preferences, so when you're setting Tags, be sure to set ones that you are likely to search for at a later date. This can be a date, a year, a person, a project, a location...anything which you think will be useful to you.

12. How do you set up the perfect Evernote user interface?

Evernote is constantly releasing options for you to change your interface to suit your personal needs. One of these is *Moleskin Notebooks* which is available to premium users – making the interface more attractive.

13. How do you convert list into checklist?

To easily convert a list into a checklist, you should first write the list, with each item on a separate line. Once you have completed your list, highlight each item, and then click the checkbox button on the top toolbar. This is the same for Windows and Mac.

14. Do you need to download the add-ons for Evernote?

Evernote works as a standalone application. However, the add-ons are there to help you get the best out of Evernote. The more productive you want to be with it, the more you'll want to download.

15. Can you try Evernote premium?

You can buy a month of Evernote premium using Evernote points, which you can earn by referring people you know to use the application. If they sign up, you will earn points. A month with all the bonus premium features will demonstrate how useful it will be to you.

CONCLUSION

So as you can see Evernote has absolutely everything you could possibly need to get organized and be more productive. Most people say that once they have adapted to using Evernote they don't know how they ever survived without it, and with all the available features it's easy to see why!

Notes can be in a variety of different formats, according to whatever you need, and these Notes can be organized by Notebooks, Stacks and Tags meaning that you never have to misplace anything ever again. The extensive search options mean that as well as being well organized, everything within Evernote is also very easy to find.

Once you get your head around the unique but easy-to-use features of Evernote, you will quickly see your time opening up, but also your space. If you start to save all your documents to Evernote, you will eventually become 'paperless' which will make your office space a lot easier to manage.

Everything about Evernote, including the add-ons, is designed with your organization and productivity in mind, and you can use the application according to your personal requirements. The fact that you can have Evernote with you on all of your devices you never have to be without it, or your to do list, again!

ABOUT THE AUTHOR

John Scott has always been a workaholic. Ambitious from a young age, he worked his way to the top of the business world, eventually becoming in charge of several businesses. As you can imagine, this kept him very busy. Every moment of the night and day was spent thinking about and trying to manage this disparate businesses and trying to keep his sanity.

Eventually, he began to realize that there must be a better way of organizing his life, thoughts, and businesses. He knew that there must be a better way to manage everything he needed to do and make sure that day-to-day activities were completed in the most efficient and effective way.

Searching the internet for solutions, he came across Evernote. At first, he just thought it was another of many cloud-based, note-taking programs, but he quickly began to realize that it was so much more than that. It was a way to master his management responsibilities, get things done faster, and even save a little bit of time for himself and his family. He finally had time to focus on the really important things–the things outside the business world where true success lies.

He quickly began studying and using this program, learning everything that he could about it. He has been using it for years and discovered every feature of this great tool. This book is a compilation of all of that knowledge.

Printed in Great Britain
by Amazon